Improving Access to Health Services for Children and Pregnant Women

Brookings Dialogues on Public Policy

The presentations and discussions at Brookings conferences and seminars often deserve wide circulation as contributions to public understanding of issues of national importance. The Brookings Dialogues on Public Policy series is intended to make such statements and commentary available to a broad and general audience, usually in summary form. The series supplements the Institution's research publications by reflecting the contrasting, often lively, and sometimes conflicting views of elected and appointed government officials, other leaders in public and private life, and scholars. In keeping with their origin and purpose, the Dialogues are not subjected to the formal review procedures established for the Institution's research publications. Brookings publishes them in the belief that they are worthy of public consideration but does not assume responsibility for their accuracy or objectivity. And, as in all Brookings publications, the judgments, conclusions, and recommendations presented in the Dialogues should not be ascribed to the trustees, officers, or other staff members of the Brookings Institution.

Improving Access to Health Services for Children and Pregnant Women

JOSHUA M. WIENER

JEANNIE ENGEL

THE BROOKINGS INSTITUTION / Washington, D.C.

Copyright © 1991 by
THE BROOKINGS INSTITUTION
1775 Massachusetts Avenue, N.W.
Washington, D.C. 20036
All rights reserved

LIBRARY OF CONGRESS CATALOG CARD NUMBER 91-076610

ISBN 0-8157-9375-8

9 8 7 6 5 4 3 2 1

About Brookings

The Brookings Institution is a private nonprofit organization devoted to research, education, and publication in economics, government, foreign policy, and the social sciences generally. Its principal purpose is to bring knowledge to bear on the current and emerging public policy problems facing the American people. In its research, Brookings functions as an independent analyst and critic, committed to publishing its findings for the information of the public. In its conferences and other activities, it serves as a bridge between scholarship and public policy, bringing new knowledge to the attention of decisionmakers and affording scholars a better insight into policy issues. Its activities are carried out through three research programs (Economic Studies, Governmental Studies, Foreign Policy Studies), a Center for Public Education, a Publications Program, and a Social Science Computation Center.

The Institution was incorporated in 1927 to merge the Institute for Government Research, founded in 1916 as the first private organization devoted to public policy issues at the national level; the Institute of Economics, established in 1922 to study economic problems; and the Robert Brookings Graduate School of Economics and Government, organized in 1924 as a pioneering experiment in training for public service. The consolidated institution was named in honor of Robert Somers Brookings (1850–1932), a St. Louis businessman whose leadership shaped the earlier organizations.

Brookings is financed largely to endowment and by the support of philanthropic foundations, corporations, and private individuals. Its funds are devoted to carrying out its own research and educational activities. It also undertakes some unclassified government contract studies, reserving the right to publish its findings.

A Board of Trustees is responsible for general supervision of the Institution, approval of fields of investigation, and safeguarding the independence of the Institution's work. The President is the chief administrative officer, responsible for formulating and coordinating policies, recommending projects, approving publications, and selecting staff.

Author's Preface

The health status of children and pregnant women in the United States is not what it should be. One reason for poor health outcomes is that children and pregnant women do not have access to basic health services. Even when financing is available, such as through the medicaid program, providers may not be available or willing to provide services. Complicating the access problem are a variety of social issues, including poverty, poor nutrition, drugs, crime, substandard housing, and unemployment. Traditional medical approaches are too narrow to address this broad array of problems. Moreover, programs that take a broader perspective are inadequately funded.

This volume, which examines many issues related to the financing and delivery of health services for pregnant women and children, reports on and amplifies presentations made at a July 1989 conference sponsored by the Brookings Institution in conjunction with the National Commission to Prevent Infant Mortality. The conference and the book owe a great deal to Rae Grad, Mary Brecht Carpenter, and Carolyn Rutsch of the commission; without their expertise and enthusiasm, neither would have come to pass. Warren I. Cikins of the Center for Public Policy Education at Brookings also provided invaluable help in organizing the conference. Carol A. Delaney and Lucinda Perry assisted in that regard and implemented conference activities.

We wish to thank the many people who provided useful comments on versions of the manuscript: Kathy J. Bryant, Ronald H. Carlson, Mary Brecht Carpenter, Janet Chapin, Richard Curtis, Rae Grad, Robert Greenstein, Katherine Harris, Catherine A. Hess, Ian Hill, Vince Hutchins, Woodrow Kessel, Bonnie Lefkowitz, Deborah Lewis-Idema, William A. Niskanen, Jackie Noyes, Alice M. Rivlin, Martha Romans, Carolyn Rutsch, Donald Schiff, Andreas Schneider, and Gail R. Wilensky. Carolyn J. Hill, E. Carole Hingleton, and Diane Maranis provided secretarial assistance, Caroline Lalire edited the manuscript, and Susan L. Woollen prepared it for typesetting.

Brookings is grateful to the following organizations for their financial support of the conference and book: National Commission to Prevent Infant Mortality, American Academy of Pediatrics, American College of Obstetricians and Gynecologists, American Hospital Association, National Perinatal Association, and Health Resources and Services Administration and Maternal and Child Health Bureau of the U.S. Department of Health and Human Services. No official endorsement by these funding organizations is either intended or should be inferred.

The views expressed in this volume are those of the authors and should not be ascribed to the persons or organizations acknowledged or to the staff members, officers, or trustees of the Brookings Institution.

Joshua M. Wiener
Jeannie Engel

October 1991
Washington, D.C.

Contents

CHAPTER ONE

Introduction

American women and children, particularly poor ones, face serious health risks. Infant mortality rates in the United States are far higher than those in nineteen other industrialized nations, including Canada, France, Germany, and Spain.[1] Infant death rates for blacks are twice those for whites.[2] The national rate of low birth weight, the factor most associated with infant mortality, has remained virtually unchanged throughout the past decade.[3] In nearly a quarter of all live births, prenatal care begins late or is not received at all.[4]

A major impediment to reducing infant mortality and improving maternal and child health in the United States is the fact that many children and pregnant women do not have access to basic health services. This lack of access to care may result in the need for expensive neonatal care and long-term interventions after the child is born. In some instances, individual behaviors such as smoking, alcohol and drug abuse, and poor nutrition contribute to high levels of infant mortality. Other risk factors associated with these high levels include early teenage childbearing, low educational attainment, and single parenthood.

Currently, health care for infants and pregnant women is financed and delivered through a variety of sources. Medicaid, the federal-state entitlement program for the poor, and special publicly funded delivery system programs, such as community health centers, provide care to the low-income population. Public and private hospitals and state and local health departments are also important providers of care to the poor. Employer-sponsored health insurance covers most people who work and their families. But despite the multiplicity of programs, many children and pregnant women do not receive basic health services.

Although gaps in financing is the dominant problem, it is not the only one. In many inner-city and rural areas, health care providers are simply not available. In other areas they are available, but care is provided in a fragmented and ineffective way. Delivery system programs, like community health centers, the National Health Service Corps, and the maternal and child health block grant program, address these problems, but their funding is limited.

Over the last several years, improving access to health services for pregnant women and children has moved up on the national political agenda. Since 1984 Congress has steadily raised medicaid eligibility ceilings for these groups and has broken the linkage to the aid to families with dependent children program. As of 1991 all states must cover pregnant women with incomes below 133 percent of the federal poverty level and children to age 6 with incomes below the poverty level. States have the option of extending medicaid coverage for infants to age 1 and pregnant women with incomes up to the 185 percent poverty level. And beginning July 1, 1991, states are required to phase in medicaid eligibility to all children up to age 19 whose family incomes are below poverty.

Besides expanding medicaid eligibility, proposals have been made to offer mandates or incentives for employers to provide health care coverage, including maternity and well-child care to workers and their dependents. Finally, to improve the health care delivery system, some have recommended increased funding for the maternal and child health block grant, community and migrant health centers, the special supplemental food program for women, infants, and children, substance abuse programs, and family planning clinics.

President George Bush has also identified this as a major domestic issue. In 1989, in response to this problem, he established a White House Task Force on Infant Mortality, chaired by James Mason, assistant secretary for health. In his 1991 State of the Union address, President Bush declared, "Good health care is every American's right and every American's responsibility."[5] The president's 1992 budget calls attention to the need to invest in children.[6]

There have also been a wide array of blue-ribbon, bipartisan commissions and reports at the national, state, and local levels calling for more investment in young children. The Committee for Economic Development, the National Commission to Prevent Infant Mortality, the Ford Foundation, the Health Policy Agenda for the American People, the National Leadership Commission on Health Care, the American Academy of Pediatrics, and the Pepper Commission, to name just a few, have all recommended increased spending for health programs for prenatal care and low-income children.[7]

To further public discussion of strategies to ensure that pregnant women and children receive access to basic health services, the Brookings Institution, in conjunction with the National Commission to Prevent Infant Mortality, held a conference on July 17, 1989, in Washington, D.C., entitled Improving Access to Health Services for Pregnant Women and Children. The purpose of the conference was to explore ways to ensure universal access to health services and to examine the need for providing services that go beyond traditional medical care to address social, informational, and behavioral problems. A list of the panel participants and a list of other attendees can be found after the appendixes. This volume reports on and amplifies the discussion at this conference.

MATERNAL AND CHILD HEALTH

In 1988 nearly 39,000 infants died before their first birthday.[8] From 1970 to 1988 the total infant mortality rate dropped from 20.0 to 10.0 per 1,000 births, and black infant mortality declined from 32.6 to 17.6 per 1,000 births.[9] But in communities where poverty has increased, drugs and AIDS are widespread, and fewer health care providers are available, the prognosis is for higher, not lower, infant mortality rates. Such cities as Washington, Philadelphia, and Baltimore have infant mortality rates that are higher than those in Bulgaria and Costa Rica.[10]

A prime factor in determining infant death and disability is low birth weight (5.5 pounds or less). Each year more than one-quarter million low-birth-weight babies are born in the United States, 6.9 percent of all live births. These babies are forty times more likely to die in their first month of life than are normal-birth-weight babies, and they are two to three times more likely to suffer chronic handicapping conditions than their heavier peers.[11] For example, children with low birth weights are 50 percent more likely to use special education programs.[12]

Over the last several years, high-technology medicine has managed to reduce the death rate for these low-birth-weight infants, even though the percentage of infants born with low birth weights has remained constant. As Joycelyn Elders, director of the Arkansas Department of Health, put it at the Brookings conference, "What we have done is to improve technology, which is not likely to advance much more in the next few years. We are going to have to do something more basic than finding a better machine."

Although there is growing recognition that prenatal care is an important component in ensuring healthy pregnancies and babies, women in the United States have poor records for participation in prenatal care. Prenatal care is especially beneficial if women begin to use services early in the pregnancy.[13] Overall, between 1980 and 1988 little progress was made in getting women into early prenatal care; roughly a quarter of live births were to women who began prenatal care in the second or third trimester.[14] This fact is disturbing because early initiation of prenatal care can reduce the incidence of low birth weights for blacks and whites.[15] Women who are poor, unmarried, under age 18, black or Hispanic, or have less than a high school education are the least likely to receive adequate prenatal care.[16]

Comprehensive prenatal care can also be cost-effective over the long run. The Institute of Medicine has estimated that for every $1.00 spent on improving prenatal care for low-income and poorly educated women, there would be a reduction in the number of low birth weights that would save $3.38 in the first year of life.[17] A study of prenatal care in New Hampshire calculated a $2.57 medical care cost saving for every $1.00 spent on prenatal care.[18] And a 1984 American Academy of Pediatrics report found that for every $1 spent on prenatal care, $2 to $10 is saved on the cost of providing neonatal intensive care and other medical care for unhealthy newborns.[19] Furthermore, in an evaluation of the federally funded nutrition program for pregnant women and children, the receipt of adequate prenatal care was associated with medicaid savings independent of participation in the nutrition program.[20]

LACK OF HEALTH COVERAGE

One of the main reasons that so many women and children do not get the health care they need is simply that they cannot afford it. In 1986, 37 million Americans under age 65 were not covered by private insurance, medicare, or medicaid. Moreover, the percentage of the population without coverage is growing, having risen from 12.5 percent in 1980 to 15.3 percent in 1986.[21] In 1985 approximately 14.5 million women of childbearing age either had no public or private health coverage or had insurance that did not cover maternity care.[22] One of five children under age 18 is poor, but in 1988 only about one-half of all poor children used medicaid to help pay for their medical care.[23] The expansions of medicaid eligibility for children mandated by the Omnibus Budget Reconciliation Act of 1990 should increase this percentage over time.

Gaps in coverage occur for several reasons. Although pregnant women and young children have been singled out for considerably improved coverage, general financial eligibility levels for medicaid are still quite low. Many people who are eligible do not apply because they do not know they are eligible or do not want to brave the application process. In terms of private insurance, most people obtain coverage through their employers, but not all employers provide insurance.

The consequences of lack of insurance or medicaid coverage can be substantial. In 1986 an estimated 14 million people had serious difficulty paying for medical care, and more than 1 million were turned away from a hospital or physician because they could not pay.[24] Hospitals, under growing pressure to hold down costs, are increasingly reluctant to provide uncompensated care, which must be passed on as a price increase to private insurers.

Not surprisingly, because of the inability to pay, the uninsured use fewer health services. In 1986 uninsured persons with less than $15,000 in family income had half as many physician contacts as the insured and used about a third fewer hospital days. Similarly, among persons in fair or poor health, the uninsured have only half the number of physician visits as the insured.[25] A recent study found that infants born to parents without health insurance were 30 percent more likely to become ill or die than those born to insured parents.[26]

Nonetheless, it is not true that the uninsured have no access to health care. Many uninsured pay out of pocket for their health care. In addition, as Lawrence Lewin, president of Lewin/ICF, argued at the conference, "Many of the uninsured have access through delivery system programs like community health centers as well as the rather sizable and often overlooked system of charity care, philanthropy, and cross subsidies that the insured population provides to the uninsured." However, these programs and indirect subsidies are unable to fill all the need, because most have funding shortfalls and the others do not constitute a "system" of care that promotes appropriate and timely use of services. Besides financial problems, the barriers to care include inadequate service capacity, deficiencies in the organization and delivery of care, and cultural and personal factors that limit care.

CONFERENCE THEMES

Improving the health status of pregnant women and children is a great challenge for the United States. Both financial and delivery system problems have impeded access to health care. Medical care is expensive, and without third-party coverage many cannot afford it, especially if serious illness strikes. Furthermore, lack of providers, poor service coordination, and multiple social problems, such as drug use, poor nutrition, and poverty, complicate the health problems of this population and the ability of the health care system to deal with them.

At the Brookings conference, the discussion focused on four interrelated themes. First, the problem of access to health services for pregnant women and children is much more complicated now than it was ten or fifteen years ago. Homelessness, AIDS, and drug abuse with far more dangerous substances are now inextricably interwoven with the more traditional problems of poverty, poor nutrition, and a fragmented health care delivery system. Meeting the needs of high-risk pregnant women and their children requires going beyond the technical provision of medical care. As such, general solutions to the problem of health care for the uninsured are not adequate to meet the complex needs of this population.

Second, in recent years the public policy debate on health care for the uninsured has focused on financing options, such as expanding medicaid and mandating private insurance. In the process, delivery system approaches, such as community and migrant health centers, the maternal and child health program, and the National Health Service Corps, have been virtually ignored. Because of the social problems alluded to earlier and the dearth of providers in inner-city and rural areas, higher priority should be given to strategies that deal comprehensively with the problems of the poor. This is not to say that financing options are wrong or unimportant, but rather that the basic approach needs to go beyond just giving people an insurance or medicaid card.

Third, the traditional dichotomies between public and private strategies and between financing and delivery options are artificial and counterproductive. No single approach can meet the needs of all people, nor is it politically possible. A comprehensive approach will require public and private initiatives that address both financing and delivery of services. The challenge is to craft proposals that build on the strengths of each and to fit them together into a whole.

Fourth, the magnitude of the infant mortality problem, the need to improve maternal and child health, and the desirability of universal access to health services are widely recognized. All too often, however, Americans view infant mortality and low birth weight as someone else's problem. They forget that these health care costs must be borne by society as a whole, either through health insurance, medicaid, or cost shifting to third-party payers. Moreover, babies who die or live with preventable disabilities adversely affect the competitiveness of our work force. As with many social policy issues, the American people see the problem but are not willing to pay the price necessary to address it.

Where there is agreement that action is necessary, there is not a clear consensus on what should be done. As Governor Lawton Chiles, chairman of the National Commission to Prevent Infant Mortality, pointed out at the conference, "Where the debate remains is on the question of who should be responsible for taking action to improve access to health care, how access to care should be implemented, and who should pay." Indeed, disagreement over the relative roles of the private and public sectors is the chief barrier to action.

CHAPTER TWO

The Social Context

Children born to women who are poor, young, minority, and under-educated and those born to women who fail to get early prenatal care are at greatest risk of infant mortality or of having long-term health problems. Barriers to improved health outcomes, especially for the poor, are more severe and more complicated than in the past because of the rise of AIDS, drug abuse, and homelessness. Attention to these new problems, however, should not overshadow other more traditional risks, like smoking and alcohol abuse, poor nutrition, and adolescent childbearing, that are associated with poor birth outcomes.

POVERTY AND ITS IMPACT ON HEALTH

Although intertwined, the problems of poverty should be somewhat separated from AIDS, drug abuse, and other social problems. Not all poor people have these behavioral problems and not all people with these behavioral problems are poor. Nonetheless, when poverty and these social problems are combined, it is especially hard to maintain healthy children and pregnant women. Reed Tuckson, health commissioner for the District of Columbia, argued at the Brookings conference that many diseases are the consequence of "how people choose to live their lives: the choices they make and the chances they take, their reaction to their environment, their sense of their own lives." Some people contend that these behaviors are the result of "lack of character" and a breakdown of moral values. Others reject this analysis, saying that it is "blaming the victim."[1] They argue that such behaviors stem from the effects of poverty, racism, hopelessness, and public neglect. For example, there is no point in blaming women for not using prenatal care in areas where few providers are available.

From a practical point of view, people must make choices among the options available to them, and poor people have fewer viable options. Because of their narrow range of options, poor people may make decisions based on day-to-day necessities and satisfactions as opposed to long-range goals. Tuckson argued that such behavior "has to do with whether or not people value their lives, whether the experience of being alive in this country has given people a sense that their lives are worthwhile and that they have a future worth planning for." Thus, he contended, African Americans, in particular, have been systematically deprived of a sense "that their lives are worthwhile by poverty and racism." Some behaviors are ways of achieving the hip and sexy life that "this country keeps on throwing at me that I am supposed to want." From a health perspective, poor nutrition, cigarette smoking, drug abuse, AIDS, and high-risk sexual activity form part of the social context in which efforts to provide care must operate.

NUTRITION

Poor nutrition is one result of the limited options available to the poor. Although improper diet can negatively affect pregnancy and birth outcomes, poor women may have other priorities. A low-income woman may choose to feed her other children before worrying about feeding herself. Fast food restaurants and the convenience stores that substitute for supermarkets in many inner-city areas usually do not carry fresh produce. And the special supplemental food program for women, infants, and children, which is designed to provide better nutrition to this group, is funded at a level that serves only about half the population at risk.[2]

CIGARETTE SMOKING

Although cigarette smoking by childbearing-age women declined slightly during the 1980s, more than one-quarter of women aged 18–44 smoked in 1987.[3] Maternal smoking increases the risk of infants being born with low birth weights. For example, the Ohio Department of Health reported that infants born to smokers were more than twice as likely to have low birth weight than infants born to nonsmokers.[4] One study estimated that the elimination of maternal smoking would lower the incidence of low birth weight by 25 percent and infant mortality by 10 percent.[5] Passive smoking also adversely affects infant health. There is a twofold increase in the incidence of respiratory disease among infants of mothers who smoke and also a higher rate of sudden infant death syndrome.[6]

DRUG ABUSE

Drug abuse rose during the 1980s, with cocaine and its smokable derivative, crack, accounting for much of the increase. Pregnant women have been part of this trend. The 1988 National Household Survey on Drug Abuse found that 9 percent of women aged 15–44 were current users of an illegal drug.[7] Similarly, a 1988 survey of thirty-six hospitals with a large number of deliveries found that 11 percent of pregnant women had exposed their fetuses to one or more illegal drugs, with cocaine and crack being the most common.[8] A study in Pinellas County, Florida, found that 15 percent of pregnant women screened in 1989 tested positive for substance abuse, with marijuana being the most commonly used drug.[9]

According to Tuckson, drug abuse contributes significantly to the District of Columbia's high infant mortality rate. He estimated that as many as a third of deliveries in some D.C. hospitals are to women who use drugs. Under the influence of drugs, pregnant women may be incapable of the rational thought necessary to seek prenatal care. Women may deny or be unaware of the damaging effects that drugs have on the fetus. For some women, the compulsion to use drugs may be stronger than their concern for their own and their baby's health.

Infants born to women who used drugs during pregnancy are more likely to be premature and have low birth weight and congenital birth defects.[10] Cocaine, for example, may cause constriction of blood vessels in the placenta and umbilical cord, which can result in a lack of oxygen and nutrients to the fetus and lead to poor fetal growth and development.[11] Because of these medical problems, hospital expenditures for drug-exposed infants are up to four times greater than those for infants with no indication of drug exposure.[12] These infants may also suffer from drug withdrawal and developmental and learning disabilities.

Drugs are not just a threat to the fetus. If parental drug use persists, parents may be incapable of providing a supportive home environment or of managing the medical and developmental treatment their young children may need. City and state officials report that prenatal drug exposure and drug-abusing families are placing increasing demands on their social welfare systems, especially foster care.[13]

Concern about the effect of drugs on the fetus has led to debate about whether severe legal sanctions should be imposed. Some have advocated jailing pregnant drug abusers to help ensure that they do not use drugs for the duration of their pregnancies.[14] Opponents of this strategy argue that it will dissuade those women most in need of care from seeking it, thus compounding the problem. Moreover, many drug treatment programs have long waiting lists, and a large number of the programs do not provide services to pregnant women.[15]

ACQUIRED IMMUNODEFICIENCY SYNDROME (AIDS)

AIDS is a debilitating and ultimately fatal disease that is caused by infection with the human immunodeficiency virus (HIV). AIDS is a major health problem in the United States which claims victims of all ages, both sexes, and all socioeconomic groups. The HIV virus is usually transmitted through an HIV-infected sexual partner or through HIV-contaminated intravenous drug needles. Slightly over half of reported cases of HIV infection among women in the United States were transmitted through intravenous drug use.[16] AIDS has become one of the ten leading causes of death among women of childbearing age, and if current trends continue, it will become one of the top five causes of death by 1991.[17] Among women, HIV infection occurs disproportionately among minorities of reproductive age who live in inner cities.[18] In 1988 the death rate for black women was nine times the rate for white women.[19] One out of every seventy-four Washington, D.C., women giving birth in 1990 was infected with the HIV virus.[20]

Between 30 and 40 percent of babies born to HIV-infected mothers develop AIDS.[21] Infection with the HIV virus may occur during pregnancy, at birth, or, very rarely, through breast feeding.[22] The Centers for Disease Control reported 1,962 cases of AIDS in children under age 5 as of July 1990.[23] Not infrequently, women who die of AIDS leave children who must be taken care of, either by other relatives or through foster care. On the basis of small area studies, an estimated

1,620 to 4,860 HIV-infected babies are born each year.[24] These babies may show symptoms of the AIDS disease at birth or, like adults, any number of years after being infected. Most HIV-infected infants who develop AIDS die within five years.[25]

For children infected by their mothers, there is evidence that early aggressive treatment can significantly improve their quality of life.[26] Through prenatal screening, children infected with or at risk of HIV infection can be identified early to allow for appropriate medical attention and other support services.

HIGH-RISK SEXUAL ACTIVITY

Sexual activity without birth control can lead to unintended pregnancies and unwanted children. Unmarried women and teenagers are at especially high risk of adverse birth outcomes. Moreover, having multiple partners increases the chance of contracting sexually transmitted diseases, such as gonorrhea, syphilis, and the HIV virus. The prevalence of unintended births is quite high, especially among teenagers and minority groups. Although about 37 percent of all births are unintended, fully 79 percent of births to women between ages 15 and 19, and 55 percent of births to blacks are not planned.[27] Unintended and teenage pregnancies do not give women and men a chance to create a financially secure home environment. Almost half of adolescent mothers had family incomes below the poverty line in 1985 and 1986—just over $600 a month for a mother with one child—and nearly two-thirds were below one and one-half times the poverty line.[28]

Teenage pregnancy is of particular concern. As Joycelyn Elders summed it up at the conference, "We have too many children having children." In 1988 almost half a million women aged 15–19 gave birth.[29] Very little progress was made in reducing birthrates for this age group during the 1980s. For teens aged 15–17, the birthrate increased 6 percent between 1987 and 1988, resulting in a rate of 33.8 per 1,000 population, which was higher than in any year since 1977.[30] Birthrates among black teens ages 15–19 were almost two and one-half times those for white teenagers. About one-sixth of Hispanic births were to teenagers in 1988, compared with one-tenth of white, non-Hispanic births and nearly one-fourth of black, non-Hispanic births.[31]

Intertwined with the problems of unintended and teenage pregnancies is the increasing proportion of births to unmarried mothers. In 1988 fully 26 percent of all births were to unmarried women, up from 18 percent in 1980.[32] Unmarried women are much more likely than married women to delay prenatal care until the third trimester or to receive no prenatal care at all.[33]

The health implications of unintended pregnancies and of teenage and unmarried parenthood are clear and negative. Women with unwanted pregnancies may not be as likely as women with desired pregnancies to practice healthy behaviors, such as eating nutritionally balanced diets, seeking prenatal care, and refraining from smoking, drinking, and taking drugs. Infants who are unplanned or unwanted have a greater risk of low birth weight. One study concluded that if all pregnancies were planned, the rate of low birth weight could be reduced by 5 percent among whites and 16 percent among blacks.[34] Overall, unmarried women are about twice as likely as married women to have low-birth-weight infants.[35] The rate of low birth weight for white unmarried women is 68 percent higher than for white married women. Among blacks, the rate is 45 percent higher for unmarried women.

CONCLUSION

The causes of ill health among children and pregnant women are deeply imbedded in the social fabric. In recent years new and complex social problems, principally AIDS and drug abuse, have been added to the traditional issues of smoking, poor nutrition, poverty, teenage pregnancy, and births to unmarried women. Referring to inner-city areas with a large collection of these problems, Edmund Haislmaier, policy analyst for the Heritage Foundation, argued at the conference that they formed "self-destructive black holes. They suck in the people who are trapped there and shut out the light, shutting out the needed services across the whole spectrum. The larger question is how to address breaking out of that cycle . . . by making fundamental reforms." Improving the health of these groups requires strategies and programs that go beyond a medical model to address the underlying social conditions.

CHAPTER THREE

The Economic and Budget Context

Improving access to health services for pregnant women and children is likely to require a big infusion of new resources. In the public sector, there are many competing demands for existing funds and a resistance to raising new revenue. Current estimates are that the fiscal 1992 federal budget deficit will be $362 billion.[1] Most economists think that reducing the deficit is critical to ensuring future economic growth.[2] Maternal and child health initiatives must compete with other programs to obtain additional funding. Even if federal taxes were raised, new revenue would probably be earmarked for deficit reduction rather than for any particular policy or program area.

Passage of the Budget Enforcement Act of 1990 further complicates the budget environment, at least through fiscal 1995.[3] The new budget rules divide spending into discretionary programs and entitlements and revenues. For fiscal 1992 and 1993, discretionary spending is subject to separate budget caps for defense, international, and domestic programs. The cap for domestic discretionary programs cannot be increased by raising taxes, cutting entitlement programs, or cutting other discretionary spending. Appropriations for specific domestic discretionary programs can be increased only by decreasing appropriations for other domestic discretionary programs, something that is likely to be extremely difficult to do. For fiscal 1994 and 1995, all discretionary spending is subject to a single overall cap, but the limit is set well below the amount needed to maintain all discretionary programs at the current level. Thus domestic programs will have to compete with military and international programs for a reduced pool of money.

For entitlement programs, such as medicaid, the new rules require that changes in these programs and in revenues combined must not increase the deficit in any year. Any entitlement program can be increased only if another entitlement is cut or if taxes or fees are raised. Similarly, a tax can be cut only if another is increased or if entitlement spending is reduced. This requirement, which is termed pay-as-you-go, applies not to each new law individually but to the total of all laws affecting a fiscal year. Again, this portion of the budget is self-contained, and cuts in discretionary spending cannot be used to fund entitlement program increases. Thus through fiscal 1995 the prospects for large increases in appropriations for programs like community health centers, the maternal and child health block grant, and medicaid seem particularly dim.

In this difficult economic and budget context, it is common for federal policymakers to voice support for improved services for pregnant women and children, yet fail to provide additional funding. Alice Rivlin, a senior fellow at Brookings, noted at the conference, "It is hard to find anybody who is against little children." Speakers generally argued in favor of increased government investment for this population both on moral grounds and as a way to improve America's future competitiveness. They differed, however, on whether the federal government or state governments should have the lead role in addressing this issue.

INCREASING DEBATE ON GOVERNMENT INVESTMENT

At the core of the debate over government policy in this area is the allocation of limited resources. Advocates of a large federal, state, and local investment in health care for children and pregnant women make three arguments. First, there are moral and humane reasons for increasing government investment in improving access to health care for children and pregnant women. The vulnerability of these groups, combined with the research evidence that early intervention can prevent long-term physical and learning disabilities, has led to widespread support for the idea of enlarging public health programs targeted to them.[4] Additionally, government has a long history of taking responsibility for the health care of the poor, either directly through the provision of services at clinics and public hospitals or indirectly through the financing of medicaid, community health centers, and other programs.

Second, the economic rationale for more public expenditures for maternal and child health care include investing in the productivity and economic well-being of future generations. At the Brookings conference, Robert Greenstein, director of the Center on Budget and Policy Priorities, argued that one route to strengthening the economy is "trying to improve the skills and capacity of our work force of tomorrow so that we will have more productive workers as our nation competes in an increasingly global economic environment." And according to Willis Goldbeck, president of the Washington Business Group on Health, "Slowly, some people in the business community are starting to recognize that investing in the future generations of Americans is nothing less than investing in your own shares on the stock market and investing in your own employment."

Poor health can lead to long-term problems that can limit a child's ability to learn in school. Poor health also keeps children home from school and prevents optimal learning. As adults, health problems increase absenteeism and divert energy from the job. Poor health inhibits work skills necessary for a future competent and competitive work force, acting as a drag on productivity and economic growth. Investing in the future generation is becoming increasingly important because fewer people are entering the labor market and future jobs will require greater skill and literacy.[5]

Third, despite the deficit, it is possible to "find room" in the budget to pay for new initiatives responsibly. Greenstein asserted that if we make health care for pregnant women and children one of our national priorities, "there really is no shortage of ways to finance this. There is a shortage of political will, but there is not a shortage of options with which to finance it." On the expenditure side, he proposed reducing spending for defense, the Economic Development Administration, Amtrak, and the Small Business Administration. On the revenue side, he suggested that consideration be given to making a greater portion of social security benefits taxable, raising income tax rates on upper-income persons, increasing estate and excise taxes, and requiring that all state and local employees pay the medicare payroll tax.

In contrast to the advocates of increased government aid, skeptics argued that major new health care initiatives are not feasible. The competing demands for government funds are too extensive: the repair of bridges, roads, and subways, deficit reduction, drug abuse enforcement and treatment, education, aid to Eastern Europe and the Soviet Union, the strategic defense initiative, savings and loan bailouts, welfare reform, and basic scientific research, among others. In addition, some observers, noting the tangled complexity of the problems of the poor, wondered whether economic development or general antipoverty programs might have a greater impact on health status than medical care programs. Closely related to this point is the general frustration over how much America spends on health care and what it gets for its money.[6] Referring to the high rate of growth in health care expenditures, William Niskanen, chairman of the Cato Institute, asserted, "We are not getting that much for our dollar. Medical care spending per person, corrected for inflation, increased about 60 percent in the last decade. That is several times the rate of growth of real income. This has got to be constrained. It has not contributed that much to our health."

Advocates of a go-slow approach also downplayed the urgency of new initiatives. Niskanen, for example, contended that "it is not obvious that a new approach is necessary to address the perceived problems of maternal and infant health care. Since the beginning of this century—long before any federal programs addressed to this condition were imagined—the infant mortality rate has declined about one-half every two decades. . . . During the most recent twenty years, the infant mortality rate has declined more than one-half, despite a small increase in the percent of children in poor families and a shocking increase in the percent of children born to single mothers, groups with much higher relative infant mortality rates. . . . The long, steady reduction in the infant mortality rate should not lead to complacency about the current rate, but it should at least mitigate any perceived sense of crisis about this condition."

FEDERAL VERSUS STATE ROLE

While there was a high degree of consensus at the Brookings conference that government programs to improve access to health care for children and pregnant women are desirable, there was less agreement on which level of government—federal, state, or local—should have primary responsibility for these expenditures. Currently, all levels of government are involved.

There are four principal reasons for a strong federal role in providing health care for pregnant women and children. First, because 37 million people are uninsured, improving access to health care is a national problem, with no state immune from the problem. Americans typically look to their national government to solve national problems. Federal action potentially allows for a faster resolution to a problem, as opposed to action by fifty different states with fifty different solutions.

Second, improving access to health care is, in part, a problem of resource redistribution. The federal government is better situated to address these issues because it can reallocate resources from upper-income people in one state to lower-income people in another state. At the extreme, reallocating resources solely within Mississippi is a futile exercise, because the state does not have enough upper-income residents to pay for what is needed. Currently, states compete for new businesses partly on how low their taxes are, a point of competition directly at odds with raising revenues for social programs. Moreover, as Greenstein pointed out at the conference, federal financing through taxes would probably be more progressive than state tax systems, which tend to rely on regressive sales and property taxes.

Third, although about half of all states have voluntarily expanded their medicaid and other programs to include a larger number of poor pregnant women and children than the minimums required by law, other states have not and will not move further without additional federal mandates. While maintenance of flexibility and diversity in how services are organized and delivered is probably desirable, no public policy goal other than states' rights is served by allowing states to cover only some of the people below a minimum financial standard. There is, after all, no disagreement over the need for coverage, nor is there much possibility that this population can obtain coverage without help.

Fourth, as many argue, access to basic health services for pregnant women and children should be a fundamental element of life: the federal government should ensure that all people are eligible on an equal basis and that access to health care should not be held hostage to a person's welfare status, employment status, or income level.

Disputing these points, Niskanen contended that the states, not the federal government, should have the lead role on this issue. Although states are having budgetary problems of their own, the federal government is clearly "broke." Moreover, he asserted, "The federal government has no resources that are not available to the sum of the states." If raising money is the problem, then the states are at least as capable as the federal government—and perhaps more capable. Thus it is "simply unrealistic to expect the federal government to fund major new initiatives." Second, the problems of providing maternal and child health are extremely diverse and subject to local objectives and conditions. "The federal government," Niskanen maintained, "has no comparative advantage in financing or providing medical care for mothers and infants. . . . There are no economies of scale in providing these services, except from some types of research that cannot be realized by the states. The services provide no obvious benefits that are external to each state." State and local governments are better able to reflect this diversity and act accordingly. Finally, Niskanen argued that there is no specific constitutional authority for direct federal maternal and child health policies and programs.

CONCLUSION

The federal budget deficit and the current economic problems of the states create an unfavorable political climate for proposals to increase government health spending for pregnant women and children. Pronouncements of concern about inadequate access to health care by public officials are often not accompanied by an increased allocation of resources. To be sure, public expenditures for health care for the low-income population in general and for pregnant women and children are already substantial, yet serious gaps remain. Public officials have implicitly decided that funding other programs or maintaining lower tax rates is preferable to increasing resources to fill the gaps in health services for children and pregnant women. Frustration with increasingly scarce resources in the public sector has heightened interest in nongovernmental strategies such as mandating larger private insurance coverage.

Resource allocation, then, is at the core of the debate about providing universal access. Advocates of increased government resources affirm the moral right to health care, stressing the vulnerability of pregnant women and children and the potential economic and social benefits of improved health status for these groups. Opponents dispute the sense of crisis and contend that these resources are better used elsewhere. To date, the advocates have won rhetorical battles, but the opponents have dominated the resource allocation war.

Beyond the level of resources is the question of what should be the roles of different levels of government. Here it seems clear to most observers that the federal, state, and local governments must all play several roles. Realistically, the problems are too large and complex and the resources too limited to assign total responsibility to any one level of government. But there may be appropriate divisions of roles. For example, it may make sense for the federal government to focus on funding, while state and local governments concentrate on organizing the delivery system.

CHAPTER FOUR

Options for Reform: Medicaid Expansions

Medicaid, the federal-state entitlement program, is the principal health care financing mechanism for the poor. In 1985 approximately 17 percent of all births were to medicaid-covered mothers.[1] In 1989 medicaid covered 16.8 million children under the age of 21 and nonelderly adults, mostly women of childbearing age.[2] For this group, medicaid spent $15.1 billion for health care services. Since 1984, raising the standards for medicaid financial eligibility and expanding the scope of services that states can or must offer have been the main strategies for improving access to health services for pregnant women and children. An evaluation by the General Accounting Office suggests that a large percentage of the women made eligible by recent medicaid expansions have, in fact, enrolled in the program.[3]

Under broad federal guidelines, states set their own eligibility levels and determine what services will be covered and how services will be reimbursed. However, as mentioned, federal law requires that states cover children up to age 6 with incomes below the poverty line and pregnant women with incomes below 133 percent of the poverty line. As a result of the Omnibus Budget Reconciliation Act of 1990, states must also, on a phased basis, provide medicaid eligibility for children between ages 6 and 19 in families below 100 percent of the poverty line. States, at their option, may cover infants and pregnant women with incomes up to 185 percent of the poverty line. A detailed history of recent changes in medicaid eligibility policy can be found in appendix A.

Medicaid has made an important contribution toward improving access to health services by the low-income population. One study found that in 1982 low-income persons living in states with extensive medicaid coverage received substantially more physician visits than low-income persons living in states with only limited medicaid programs (or Arizona, which did not have a medicaid program at that time).[4] Although recent survey data indicate that, overall, African-Americans use health services less frequently than the white population,[5] Link and others found that black and white medicaid recipients have basically the same use of ambulatory care services.[6] Similarly, in 1983 low-income children covered by medicaid were more likely to receive well-child care than low-income children not covered by medicaid.[7]

Medicaid has several major advantages as a method of financing health services for pregnant women and children over other approaches. Ian Hill, health policy analyst at the National Governors' Association, noted at the conference that, as an entitlement program, medicaid is obligated to pay for certain services to all people who meet the eligibility standards and manage to obtain services. Neither the federal nor state governments can limit expenditures simply by setting appropriations at an arbitrary level. In the 1980s, he said, entitlement programs have had better luck than appropriated programs in obtaining additional funds.[8] And since medicaid is a "sophisticated financing system existing in all states," it provides a national structure that touches every part of the country. Relatedly, because of its national structure and its reliance on existing providers, the number of people eligible to receive services can be expanded fairly quickly by changing the financial eligibility criteria. Finally, since expenditures are shared between the federal and state governments, the medicaid program can leverage federal money by combining with state dollars.

OPTIONS FOR REFORM

The medicaid expansions of the 1980s have severed the ties between the receipt of cash assistance and medicaid eligibility for poor pregnant women and young children. For advocates of medicaid eligibility expansions for this population, there are two broad options for additional action.

The first option is to build on the basic strategy that has characterized federal initiatives since 1984. Efforts in this area would include raising the percent of the poverty line under which pregnant women and children could qualify for medicaid and raising the children's maximum age for eligibility. This option has the advantage of being fairly simple to legislate and administer.

An alternative approach, suggested at the conference by Gail Wilensky, vice president of Project HOPE, would be to establish a "medicaid buy-in" program for the lower-income population. As described by Wilensky, "The notion is that, rather than have the all-or-nothing eligibility for medicaid beyond which you have no provision of services at all, we try to make more gradual transitions off medicaid so that individuals would be responsible for paying some share and a gradually increasing share of the actuarial value of a medicaid program." Using a voucher that was inversely related to income, individuals (and their employers) could purchase medicaid coverage. This would allow for coverage of persons not otherwise eligible for medicaid and would allow for a gradual transition off the program. To be workable, however, the level of government subsidy in the voucher would need to be quite large because per capita health care costs are high and the income of this population is low.[9]

Under either approach, medicaid expenditures would increase.[10] States' resistance to additional federal mandates has escalated over the last few years. Besides mandates on maternal and child health, recent federal requirements have been imposed on the states in the areas of improving the quality of nursing home care, medicaid coverage of elderly medicare patients, and welfare reform. All these mandates cost money, and states have argued that the federal government is asking the states to finance programs that it wants but is unwilling to pay for. This concern, however, is only partly true because medicaid is a joint federal-state financed program. Indeed, the federal government pays for slightly over half of medicaid expenditures. Nonetheless, because they are increasingly in a fiscal bind, states have difficulty financing existing programs, let alone new initiatives.[11]

ADDRESSING ISSUES IN MEDICAID

Although medicaid has many strengths, it has traditionally had problems that hamper its ability to ensure access to care. These include lack of outreach to potentially eligible people, complicated enrollment procedures, and low physician participation in medicaid. Congress and many states are moving to address these shortcomings, often in collaboration with state maternal and child health agencies. Thus these new initiatives are starting to change medicaid's traditionally passive, "bill payer" posture into a more pro-active stance. These initiatives may be particularly important if medicaid is to reach the working poor, who have traditionally not been eligible for medicaid or welfare. A detailed description of state initiatives is presented in appendix B.

Outreach and Expedited Enrollment

Medicaid does not usually encourage potentially eligible persons to enroll. Traditionally, it just processes applications of those who submit them. Moreover, as a means-tested program historically linked to cash assistance, medicaid has always sought to prevent persons who were not financially eligible from receiving benefits. Not surprisingly, the standard applications for aid to families with dependent children and for medicaid are long and difficult. According to Hill, "AFDC data show that 60 percent of all people who are denied medicaid eligibility are not rejected because of excess income or resources, but because of procedural noncompliance because of failure to keep appointments, and because of the inability to produce financial documents."

In terms of meeting the health needs of pregnant women and children, this arduous process has been counterproductive. More liberal financial eligibility standards are useless if people do not apply for benefits. Besides being deterred by the application process, families may be unaware of their eligibility. This is not surprising given the usual complexity and variability of eligibility rules among the states.

Congress and the states are addressing the problems of finding and enrolling eligible pregnant women and children by using new outreach mechanisms and by making it easier to apply for medicaid. In contrast to their normal posture, states are actually encouraging pregnant women and children to apply for medicaid by making the process quicker and easier.

First, as of January 1991, forty-six states have simplified financial eligibility standards for pregnant women by establishing maximum levels only for income, not for assets.[12] Similarly, in the Omnibus Budget Reconciliation Act of 1990, Congress mandated coverage for all children below the poverty line, regardless of family asset levels.

Second, as of January 1991, about one-half of the states have shortened their application forms, gathering only the most essential income and family information necessary to determine eligibility for pregnant women.[13] In thirteen states, final eligibility determinations must be made within a specified period of time, most commonly five to ten days.[14]

Third, as of January 1991, twenty-six states have used "presumptive eligibility" for medicaid eligibility for pregnant women, granting immediate, short-term medicaid coverage to pregnant women while they wait for definitive determinations of their financial eligibility.[15] From the providers' perspective, a key benefit of presumptive eligibility is that it guarantees reimbursement for services until permanent eligibility has been determined. But from the point of view of medicaid administrators, Hill said, making medicaid easier to obtain and making sure that only financially qualified people become eligible embraces contradictory goals that are difficult to balance.

Fourth, besides easing the application process, states have also been developing mechanisms to ensure that pregnant women do not lose eligibility. Periodic eligibility redeterminations, as required by each state for medicaid beneficiaries, can result in a temporary loss of eligibility, usually because of failure to comply with procedural requirements. This not only disrupts the continuity of care but also creates administrative problems and paperwork for providers. The Omnibus Budget Reconciliation Act of 1990 mandates continuous medicaid eligibility for pregnant women through sixty days after delivery, regardless of fluctuations in financial status.

Fifth, states are doing outreach to overcome the barriers that discourage the use of prenatal, maternity, and child care services. The Omnibus Budget Reconciliation Act of 1990 mandated the use of outreach and shortened application forms at various locations, including community health centers and hospitals serving a disproportionate number of low-income patients. Doing initial intake for medicaid at health clinics and hospitals, rather than at the welfare office, makes it easier for pregnant women and mothers to apply. States are also using several other strategies to identify potentially eligible pregnant women, including toll-free telephone hotlines, radio and television commercials, public health nurses, and community workers.

Enlarging the Scope of Services

Medicaid programs rely primarily on the existing delivery system to provide care. Unfortunately, this system is fragmented, with health, nutrition, and other services not well integrated. Working with federal and state maternal and child health programs (title V), most state medicaid programs are attempting to better coordinate their prenatal care programs with the special supplemental food program for women, infants, and children.

Coordinated care systems aim to provide accessible and comprehensive services for medical, social, psychosocial, financial, and nutritional needs. Patient advocates are assigned to help with the eligibility process, and transportation assistance is provided. Case managers can make appointments with providers for patients and follow-up to make sure the appointments are kept. In addition, nonmedical services such as nutrition counseling, parenting and childbirth education, and psychosocial counseling are provided, with some states covering home-visiting services for pregnant women as well. Home visiting is a promising strategy for delivering or improving access to early intervention services, such as prenatal and infant health care, that can help at-risk families become healthier and more self-sufficient.[16]

Two other recent legislative changes expand the scope of services available to medicaid beneficiaries. First, the Medicare Catastrophic Coverage Act of 1988 prohibits states from placing limits on the length of coverage for infants who are cared for in hospitals that serve a disproportionately large share of low-income patients. Thus states that fail to develop effective maternal and infant care programs are not able to shift the costs of caring for those patients onto providers. Second, the Omnibus Budget Reconciliation Act of 1989 requires states to cover the treatment of problems identified in childhood health screenings even if the state does not normally cover those services in its medicaid program. As a result, children are entitled to the fullest possible range of services.

Physician Participation in Medicaid

One of medicaid's most persistent problems is the shortage of physicians willing to accept medicaid patients. At the conference, Janet Perloff, associate professor at the University of Illinois at Chicago, maintained that the goal of "ensuring access to mainstream care cannot be attained if private, office-based physicians are unwilling to accept medicaid recipients."[17] Although participation is a problem across most specialties, it is especially acute for obstetrical services and is a growing problem for pediatrics. In a 1988 survey by the National Governors' Association, nearly two-thirds of state medicaid agencies reported experiencing significant problems in provider participation for maternity care.[18] A 1989 survey by the American Academy of Pediatrics found that between 1978 and 1989 the percentage of pediatricians willing to treat any medicaid patients declined from 85 percent to 77 percent.[19]

Two commonly cited reasons for low participation are malpractice concerns and low reimbursement rates. Malpractice insurance rates for obstetricians have been increasing rapidly and reached an average of $37,000 a year in 1987.[20] The number of claims against obstetrician-gynecologists (ob-gyns) is currently two to three times greater than the average for all other physicians and is comparable only to the number in a handful of other high-risk surgical specialties.[21]

These malpractice concerns have led some physicians to restrict or eliminate their maternity care. According to a 1987 survey by the American College of Obstetricians and Gynecologists, 12 percent of ob-gyns reported that they had ceased obstetrical practice, and another 13 percent had reduced their number of deliveries because of malpractice concerns.[22] Moreover, according to the Institute of Medicine, "the effects of professional liability concerns in obstetrics are being disproportionately experienced by poor women and women whose obstetrical care is financed by medicaid or provided by Community and Migrant Health Centers, and . . . this problem is, in turn, exacerbating the long-standing problems of financing and delivering obstetrical care to poor women."[23] In a study of physicians in Washington State, ob-gyns who quit the obstetric portion of their practice had a higher rate of malpractice claims than did those who continued this portion of their practice.[24] Although the research evidence is mixed, physicians widely believe that the poor are more likely to sue than the nonpoor.[25]

Low medicaid reimbursement rates are often identified as a strong deterrent to physician participation. The average medicaid obstetrical fee in 1989 was approximately 56 percent of the average national prevailing charge.[26] In 1988 over half of state medicaid agencies identified payment levels as a primary reason for low physician participation.[27] Raising medicaid reimbursement rates is often proposed as a way of improving physician participation.[28] In an effort to improve obstetric and pediatric participation, several provisions in the Omnibus Budget Reconciliation Act of 1989 require the states to make "sufficient payments" to those providers. The law obliges states to demonstrate that obstetric and pediatric services are available to medicaid recipients at least to the extent that such services are available to the general public.

At the conference, Perloff argued that the problems of provider participation are more fundamental than just reimbursement and malpractice. They have to do with the uneven geographic distribution of providers. "In many rural communities and in our nation's inner cities," she said, "the access problem is not so much one of unwillingness of physicians to participate in medicaid. Rather, the access problem stems from a lack of physicians. Even though certified nurse midwives and nurse practitioners often are more willing to care for low-income patients, their overall numbers are not large enough to meet the need. As a result, even if all pregnant women are eventually made eligible for maternity care—whether through medicaid or through some alternative financing system—some subgroups of women will be unable to convert their eligibility into access to maternity care."

In rural Illinois, although most obstetrician-gynecologists accepted medicaid patients in significant numbers, more than half of the state's counties had no ob-gyn physicians. In the city of Chicago, ob-gyns tend to locate in the more prosperous areas. According to Perloff, "In 1986 fewer than one-third of those ob-gyns located in prosperous areas accepted medicaid, while virtually all of those located in Chicago's inner city participated in medicaid." Because relatively few women eligible for medicaid reside in the prosperous areas, those who do have better access to maternity care despite lower physician participation rates.

Medicaid eligibility expansions may increase this disparity in access to medicaid participating physicians. In all likelihood, there will be more eligible people but the same number of physicians practicing in poor areas. According to Perloff, "In urban underclass areas, medicaid eligibility expansions are likely to have the effect of lengthening queues in physicians' offices without appreciably improving access. The small number of high-volume obstetrics practices found in inner-city Chicago leads us to predict that there are too few office-based physicians [in those] communities to absorb all of the additional maternity patients."

Beyond medicaid reimbursement levels, there are several deep-rooted problems that lead physicians to avoid low-income areas. Poor people tend to live in areas that have high crime and drug use and that are often physically unattractive. Language differences mean that communicating even simple instructions to patients can be difficult. Moreover, in some cases, racial discrimination by physicians may play a part.[29] According to Perloff, "If we are committed to improving access to maternity care in the inner city, we need to look well beyond eligibility and reimbursement increases to strategies which will increase the supply of providers in these communities."

CONCLUSION

Medicaid is by far the largest source of health care financing for the poor. Its main strength is that, as an open-ended entitlement program depending on the existing system of providers, the number of persons covered by the program can be rapidly increased. Recent initiatives to improve access to health services for children and pregnant women have focused on expanding medicaid eligibility. To serve these groups, several states, in some cases prodded by Congress, have altered their traditional posture and have aggressively conducted outreach, expedited enrollment, guaranteed periods of eligibility regardless of fluctuations in income, and attempted to coordinate services.

Unfortunately, medicaid's dependence on the existing health care delivery system is its greatest weakness as well as its greatest strength. The current system lacks physicians, nurse-midwives, and other practitioners in both rural areas and the inner cities. The delivery system is fragmented and is not geared to provide comprehensive services. Thus some newly eligible medicaid beneficiaries have difficulty making their medicaid card produce improved access to services. Future medicaid eligibility expansions will therefore need to cope directly with the supply of health care services. Political resistance by states to additional mandates from the federal government further compounds the difficulties of relying solely on medicaid expansions to achieve universal access.

CHAPTER FIVE

Options for Reform: Private Insurance

The majority of working-age Americans and their spouses and children have private health insurance. In 1988 approximately 75 percent of the nonelderly population had private health insurance, mostly through policies sponsored and paid for by employers.[1] Among some groups, coverage is not so widespread. For example, only 42 percent of children under age 18 in families below 200 percent of the poverty line had private insurance coverage.[2] Having health insurance, however, does not guarantee adequate coverage, since not all policies include coverage for maternity services or preventive services for infants and children.[3]

The uninsured, who constitute 16 percent of the nonelderly population, are surprisingly well integrated into the work force.[4] In 1988 fully 85 percent of the uninsured were members of a family in which someone worked.[5] Indeed, nearly two-thirds of the uninsured were in families of year-round, steadily employed workers. About half of the uninsured were in families of full-time, full-year workers who reported no unemployment during the year.[6]

The observation that most Americans receive their health coverage through their jobs and that a high percentage of the uninsured are in the work force has led to many proposals to increase private insurance coverage through the provision of employer-sponsored and employer-paid health policies. The principal advantages of this approach are that the bulk of the costs do not appear on the federal or state budgets, work incentives are strengthened, there is no welfare stigma, and flexibility in policy designs is retained. Not only do privately insured patients enjoy better overall access to the health care system than do medicaid and uninsured patients, but they also receive more services after gaining entry to the system.[7] As Lawrence Lewin noted at the Brookings conference, these strategies for covering the uninsured by providing private insurance build on existing arrangements rather than try "to wipe the slate clean."

OPTIONS

The options for increasing private coverage can be divided into proposals that provide incentives for employers to offer private insurance and those that mandate it. Although conceptually separate, many of the proposals for employer mandates include elements of the incentive strategy.

Incentive Strategies

At the heart of the incentive strategy is the belief that fringe benefits should be encouraged rather than mandated by the government. The incentive approach is supported by the Health Insurance Association of America, the Chamber of Commerce, and the National Federation of Independent Business (NFIB), among others. The key questions about this approach are how effective incentives can be at reducing the number of uninsured and at what cost to the government.

At the conference, Gail Wilensky suggested several ways of facilitating employer-sponsored health insurance. First, federal and state governments could allow tax deductions or credits for the cost of health insurance for individuals who are self-employed or sole proprietors. Approximately 7 percent of the uninsured are self-employed.[8] And to help new firms through the start-up period, time-limited tax credits could be provided.

Second, Wilensky suggested that the government provide a brokering function to help small employers who may have difficulty securing insurance plans. The administrative problems of dealing with insurers can be a serious barrier to small firms that do not have the time or staff to devote to negotiating insurance contracts. In a survey of small businesses by the NFIB Foundation, nearly a fifth of small businesses that did not offer health insurance said they would do so if the administrative "hassle" could be reduced.[9]

Third, she suggested establishing insurance pools that would combine a large number of small businesses. This would provide insurers with more people over whom to spread health care costs, thus stabilizing premiums. Under the current system, a single large expenditure by an employee of a small firm can cause health insurance premiums to skyrocket. By forming a larger pool, small businesses can benefit from the administrative, premium, and other cost savings realized by bigger businesses.

Similarly, administrative mechanisms modeled on the Taft-Hartley trusts could be developed for employees who work in high-turnover industries. These provide a way for employees to maintain health and pension benefits while moving from employer to employer. Employers pay into the trust according to the number of hours employees work. A comparable arrangement could be developed for other workers who change jobs frequently.

A related strategy is to allow small employers to purchase "bare bones" health insurance. To cut the cost of health insurance premiums, new laws in Virginia, Washington, and Florida exempt small group policies from requirements to cover certain medical treatments, such as treatment for drug and alcohol abuse, mammograms, and psychiatric care.[10]

Mandatory Strategy

The basic premise of this approach is that voluntary incentives, by themselves, will fail to reduce the number of uninsured significantly. Therefore, mandatory approaches are necessary. The mandatory strategy is supported by the Pepper Commission, the National Leadership Commission on Health Care, the American Medical Association, the Catholic Health Association, and the American Academy of Pediatrics, among others.[11] Legislation to implement this type of proposal has been introduced by Senator Edward Kennedy and Representative Henry Waxman. The state of Hawaii has mandated health insurance for employees since 1975.[12] A version of this option was adopted but not implemented in Massachusetts.[13] A similar proposal has been put forward for New York State.[14] The key question for this approach is how substantial the economic burden of mandated health insurance will be.

The American Academy of Pediatrics has developed a proposal that was described at the conference by Lawrence Lewin.[15] Under this proposal, there would be a statutory entitlement to a standard benefit package of insurance for all children through age 21 and pregnant women. All employers would either have to give children and pregnant women an insurance policy that provided specific minimum benefits or have to pay a payroll tax into a state-administered insurance fund. This requirement for employers to pay a tax or to offer insurance directly is often referred to as a "pay or play" provision.

The state-administered insurance fund would be financed through a combination of employer payroll taxes, individual premium payments, and federal and state funds now expended under medicaid for children and pregnant women. Current medicaid beneficiaries would receive private insurance through the state-administered insurance fund. Families with incomes below 133 percent of poverty would receive free care; premiums would be paid on a sliding scale for families with incomes between 133 and 200 percent of poverty.

The standard benefit package would contain three "baskets" of services, each with a different copayment rate and philosophy of use. One basket would include preventive services, such as prenatal care and well-baby care. To encourage use, no copayments or deductibles would be allowed. Another basket would contain primary care and major medical benefits, including care for acute and chronic illness, hospital care, subspecialty consultations, emergency room care, drugs, and laboratory tests. To control use and decrease the cost of premiums, there would be a deductible of $200 and a coinsurance of 20 percent for these services. The final basket would include extended major medical benefits, such as mental health care and the treatment of developmental and learning disabilities. This group of services are potentially very expensive and would be subject to strong cost containment initiatives, including case management, copayments, and a limit on benefits. There would be a catastrophic limit on out-of-pocket expenses for enrollees in both systems. Copayments and deductibles for families with incomes below 200 percent of poverty would be partly subsidized by the state-administered insurance fund.

ISSUES IN EXPANDING PRIVATE INSURANCE

In assessing options to expand private insurance, at least four issues must be considered. First, the more people who have private insurance, the less need there is for providers to shift uncompensated care costs to third-party payers. Second, without large public subsidies, private insurance may mean heavy economic burdens for small businesses. Third, private insurance, by itself, is inflationary and may add to the whole problem of escalating health care costs. And finally, the market for private health insurance is disintegrating rapidly, especially for small employers. Thus these proposals build on the weakest parts of the health insurance market.

Cost Shifting

Under the current system, the uninsured receive fewer services than the insured, but they do receive some services. For example, an insured person in fair or poor health had an average of 11.9 physician visits a year in 1986; an uninsured person with a similar health status had 5.6 physician visits a year.[16] The uninsured often do not pay for these services, or at least do not pay for them in full. Typically, health care providers charge people with insurance more than their cost of care in order to cover the shortfall from providing care to the uninsured, a process known as "cost shifting." Thus society is already incurring part of the costs of providing care to the uninsured.

Two consequences flow from the fact that the uninsured receive some health care. First, providing health insurance to the uninsured would reduce cost shifting because each person would have his or her medical expenditures covered by insurance. As the "free rider" problem is minimized, the pressure to increase insurance premiums to subsidize the uninsured would decline. Moreover, companies would no longer compete partly on whether or not their labor costs included health insurance. Second, the incremental costs to the health care system of providing insurance to the uninsured would be less than the total costs of providing care to the uninsured. Thus from a societal perspective, achieving full insurance is more affordable, because only the incremental services must be newly financed.[17]

The Cost of Mandating Employer-Sponsored Insurance

In the current government fiscal environment, encouraging or mandating private insurance is politically attractive because employers and employees, not the government, would shoulder the additional costs. Although the "off budget" nature of expenditures is seen as an advantage to proponents of mandated benefits, it is a major disadvantage to its opponents. According to Wilensky, putting the government in the position of mandating benefits, but not paying for them, eliminates the normal political constraints and accountability posed by the need to either raise taxes or cut other government activities to pay for new programs.[18]

Providing health insurance to currently uninsured employees would greatly increase labor costs. Mandating health insurance would impose new financial burdens mostly on small businesses, since almost all large firms already provide health insurance.[19] In 1988 nearly one-half of uninsured workers were employed in firms with fewer than 25 workers or were self-employed, and two-thirds worked in firms with fewer than 100 workers.[20] In a survey of small businesses, 65 percent of those who did not offer health insurance listed "high cost" as a reason.[21]

Opponents of mandates fear that requiring health insurance would raise labor costs to the point where a business would become unprofitable or be forced to lay off workers, and it would discourage the development of new small businesses.[22] According to Wilensky, incentive rather than mandating strategies "carry with them far smaller downside risks in terms of what they may do to vulnerable small employers, as well as what they may do for part-time workers, who after all, are not going to be very benefited if they don't have a job."

Surveys of businesses suggest that the possible adverse economic effects are not a trivial concern. Thirty-five percent of businesses polled by the National Association of Manufacturers indicated that they would stop hiring part-time workers (or reduce part-time hours) if health insurance benefits were mandated for this group.[23] In a survey of small businesses, 62 percent reported that they would respond to mandated benefits by increasing prices, and 73 percent said they would cut or hold down employee wage increases.[24] If health insurance comes at the expense of reduced wages, then it represents a per capita "tax" on low-income employees, which is especially regressive because employees pay the same premium regardless of income. Moreover, a quarter of small businesses polled said they would eliminate part-time jobs, and almost an eighth said they would also cut full-time jobs.

Several widely divergent estimates have been made of the potential effect on employment of mandated health insurance. At the low end, the U.S. Bipartisan Commission on Comprehensive Health Care estimated that its proposal would result in 25,000 to 50,000 fewer jobs for lower-income workers.[25] In evaluating the Kennedy-Waxman bill, Data Resources, Inc., estimated that 100,000 to 120,000 jobs would be lost, adding negligibly to the unemployment rate.[26] Moreover, some analysts have suggested that the new health expenditures and the reduced health insurance premiums for employers already providing health insurance would have an employment-stimulating effect. At the other end of the spectrum, Robbins and Robbins estimated that an employer minimum health plan would result in a loss of 1 million jobs.[27] Similarly, Monheit and Short estimated that mandated health benefits would "jeopardize the jobs" of 847,000 workers.[28]

Cushioning the economic burden through tax breaks for employers may be the only way to make expanding employer-based health insurance a politically viable option on either a mandatory or a voluntary basis.[29] However, to avoid increasing the already too large federal deficit, tax expenditures would have to be matched by increases in some other tax or reductions in other government spending. Unfortunately, these tax subsidies for small employers lessen one of the great appeals of private insurance—that taxes do not have to be increased.

Health Care Cost Control

The strategy of relying on private insurance largely takes the current delivery and financing system as given. One potential problem is that providing more people with health insurance could exacerbate the already large cost-increasing pressures in health care. The prevalence of third-party payments in health care is often cited as a cause of spiraling health care costs. National health expenditures increased from $249 billion in 1980 to $540 billion in 1988, at an average annual rate of increase of more than 10 percent a year.[30] Over that same period, health care spending increased from 9.1 percent to 11.1 percent of the gross national product. Without major new cost controls, increasing the number of insured will raise health care expenditures and fuel inflationary pressures.[31] With that in mind, at least some proposals for expanding private insurance call for the heavy use of health maintenance organizations or single-payer mechanisms to control costs.[32]

Deteriorating Market for Private Insurance

Options designed to increase the number of people with private insurance depend on its availability and affordability. In fact, the market for health insurance, especially for small businesses, has deteriorated substantially over the last few years.[33] Health care cost increases during the 1980s led to increased price competition among insurers. Health insurers, unable to control the price or volume of services, increasingly seek to offer lower premiums by insuring only healthy people. Waiting periods, preexisting condition exclusions, and the "redlining" of entire industries are now commonplace in health insurance policies, especially those offered to small businesses.

A wholesale decline in the availability of community-rated health insurance products occurred during the 1980s.[34] Under community rating, health insurance premiums are based on the average cost of the health care used by all subscribers. The premiums do not vary for subscribers in a particular geographic area, industry, or firm. When community-rated health insurance was widely available, a small firm could obtain insurance with a premium that was not adjusted for such factors as its own claims history, the health status of individual workers, and their age or occupation.

Over time, commercial insurers selected firms that were better risks and offered them lower rates, based on their own claims history. As the community-rated pool shrunk and rates rose for firms remaining in it, commercial insurance companies continued to siphon off remaining firms with the lowest health care costs. The ability to spread risk in the pool diminished as community-rated insurance products became less available. Experience-rated health insurance displaced community-rated products.

The basic problem is that the smaller the firm, the more difficult it is to pool risks through insurance, in which the losses of a few are shared among the many. In small firms, one or two employees with serious illnesses will lead to very large premium increases. The decline of community rating has adversely affected small firms whose employees have higher than average medical costs.

Competition among insurers to lower premiums by covering only healthy people has led to several exclusionary practices.[35] Medical underwriting often results in the exclusion of employees from coverage if they have preexisting conditions such as pregnancy, cancer, diabetes, heart disease, or other high-cost conditions.[36] In some cases, such persons may be denied any coverage; in others, only the specific preexisting condition is excluded. Medical underwriting may also limit the coverage available to spouses and dependents of the employee. Moreover, small companies in entire industries are sometimes excluded from coverage by insurers. Among the many types of businesses that insurers exclude are logging, mining and roofing companies, taverns, hair stylists, and medical offices.[37]

So far, efforts to address the deteriorating market have had limited success. According to Wilensky, some states have responded to the problem of the medically uninsurable by developing risk pools to provide coverage for people unable to purchase insurance because of preexisting medical conditions.[38] Most existing programs, however, have left these people with very high premiums and cost-sharing. Multiple-employer trusts face the same problems of adverse selection experienced elsewhere in the marketplace.[39] Also, to the extent that a pool is formed for insurance purposes only, companies can come and go, depending on whether less costly insurance is available to them elsewhere. If enough do leave, the pool itself can be destroyed.

Several proposals to reform the health insurance market, especially for small employers, have been put forward. For example, the Health Insurance Association of America has proposed that states prohibit insurers that sell to small employers (a business with between three and twenty-five employees) from excluding individuals from the group because of their medical risks, canceling a policy because of the deteriorating health of the insured, and imposing more than one period of preexisting-condition exclusions.[40] Under this proposal, insurance carriers would be required to limit how much their rates could vary for groups similar in geography, demographic composition, and plan design. To facilitate these reforms, the Health Insurance Association of America also proposes a private, marketwide reinsurance system to spread the risk.

CONCLUSION

Most Americans receive their health care through private health insurance sponsored, and usually paid for, by their employers. However, not all employers offer health insurance. Indeed, most of the uninsured either work or are dependents of persons who work.

Several proposals have been put forward either to mandate that employers provide health insurance or to provide incentives for employers to do so. These two approaches would clearly integrate the uninsured into mainstream medicine. But again, for vulnerable populations like low-income women and their children, health insurance does not guarantee that health care is available or accessible.

The difficulty with incentives is that it is uncertain whether they will significantly reduce the number of uninsured. Also, the more that employers receive tax breaks for offering health insurance, the more costly the program becomes to the government, thus undermining one of the main political advantages of private insurance. The difficulty with mandates is that they may impose unacceptably high economic burdens on small businesses that will result in lower wages and less employment for mostly lower-wage employees. A problem for both approaches is the rapidly deteriorating market for private health insurance among small businesses. As a result, these approaches place heavy additional burdens on the weakest part of the health insurance market.

CHAPTER SIX

Options for Reform: Delivery System

Financing strategies, such as expanding medicaid eligibility and private employer-based health insurance, can go a long way toward improving access to health services. Nonetheless, nonfinancial barriers still prevent many people from receiving adequate care. For example, in a 1986–87 study of thirty-two communities, the General Accounting Office found that the prenatal care experience of medicaid-eligible pregnant women was poor and not much better than that of the uninsured.[1] In another study, a modest increase in medicaid enrollment in Tennessee between 1984 and 1987 did not result in substantial improvements in the use of early prenatal care, in birth weight, or in neonatal mortality.[2]

In addition to financial problems, the barriers to care can be grouped into three categories.[3] First, there is an inadequate service capacity in some parts of the health care system, especially in rural areas and the inner cities. In many of these areas, there are very few physicians or other providers. Second, there are problems in the organization, practice, and atmosphere of care provided to children and pregnant women. Common barriers include inadequate coordination of services, transportation difficulties, problems in arranging child care, service hours that are inconvenient for women who work, long waits in clinics, and language barriers and other communication problems. Finally, there are cultural and personal factors that limit care. The use of prenatal care can be diminished by attitudes toward pregnancy and the importance of health care, cultural values and beliefs, different life-styles, and other psychological characteristics. In particular, pregnant women who are unaware that behavior such as drug and alcohol abuse, heavy smoking, and poor eating habits places their health and that of their babies at risk may avoid care because they anticipate that they will be pressured to change.

In order to address these problems, delivery system reform is needed as well as financing changes. For example, Gail Wilensky has argued that "for some populations—those who are difficult to reach or who have special needs, such as the homeless or the high-risk pre-natal population—specially targeted programs directed toward providers who are trained and equipped to deal with special populations are likely to be more efficient and effective than generalized insurance programs."[4]

There are two broad options for delivery system reform. First, on an incremental basis, federal and state funding for current programs can be increased. This option builds on the existing administrative structure and leaves existing financing systems in place. Second, a much more radical approach to reform would be to consciously make these programs the primary providers of health care for the poor.[5] This would be accomplished by accepting, even institutionalizing, a "two-class" system of care. In this option, direct, organized service programs specializing in treatment of the poor would be the primary sources of care for the low-income population.[6]

CURRENT PROGRAMS

A variety of federal and state programs have been designed to address delivery system problems so as to improve access to health services. At the federal level, these include the community and migrant health center (C/MHC) program, the National Health Service Corps (NHSC), the maternal and child health block grant (MCH) program, the title X family planning program, and the special supplemental program for women, infants, and children (WIC). Some of these programs are also administered with matching state funds. At the local level, health departments, public hospitals, voluntary organizations, and school-based programs are providing access to basic health services oriented toward the disadvantaged.

Maternal and Child Health Block Grant

The basic goal of the maternal and child health block grant program is to improve the health of mothers and children, particularly those with low income or limited access to services. Through funds offered by the program, states provide and facilitate access to a wide range of maternal and child health services. In fiscal 1987 more than 500,000 women received prenatal care that was at least partly subsidized by state maternal and child health programs.[7]

The emphasis of the MCH program is on building comprehensive systems of care that are family oriented and community based and that entail a partnership of public and private providers and agencies. Although states still have considerable flexibility in administering the programs, which allows them to focus on unique problems within their jurisdiction, the Omnibus Budget Reconciliation Act of 1989 amended the authorizing legislation. There are now certain requirements regarding how funds should be spent and mandated reporting on how the program is achieving goals specified in the annual state application for funds.

Eighty-five percent of the funds are allocated to the states, with states matching $3 for every $4 in federal funds provided. The remaining 15 percent of the funds provide discretionary funding to projects that address training, hemophilia diagnosis and treatment, genetic screening, and a broad range of other topics.

At the federal level, the program is administered by the Maternal and Child Health Bureau of the Public Health Service of the Department of Health and Human Services. At the state level, programs are administered by the health department.

Community and Migrant Health Centers

Beginning in 1965 as an eight-site demonstration project, there are now six hundred federally supported community and migrant health centers that serve more than 5.5 million poor people.[8] Authorized by sections 330 and 329, respectively, of the Public Health Service Act, community and migrant health centers provide primary care in a managed care system that includes support for and referral to social and other services. Health centers provide care to 1.3 million women of childbearing age and 2.1 million children under age 15.[9]

In 1987 Congress passed legislation enacting the comprehensive perinatal care program to improve the maternal and infant health care and outreach capabilities in community and migrant health centers. For fiscal 1988 Congress appropriated approximately $20 million to expand C/MHC perinatal capacity, which grew to $31.6 million in fiscal 1990.[10] These funds allowed C/MHCs to increase outreach and case management activities during pregnancy and the first year of life. These services have reached approximately 100,000 mother-infant pairs.[11] Congress has also established a small health care program for the homeless through the community health centers.

Federal appropriations for community and migrant health centers were $475 million in fiscal 1990, accounting for about 40 percent of total operating costs.[12] Medicaid, medicare, private insurance, and state, local, and other sources provide the balance. Reflecting a federal reluctance to fund service programs directly, the relative share of expenses paid by federal grant money has declined sharply, and state and local sources have increased somewhat over the last few years.

At the federal level, the community and migrant health center program is administered by the Public Health Service's Bureau of Health Care Delivery and Assistance (BHCDA) in the Department of Health and Human Services. Because it is a direct grant program to the centers, state governments are not directly responsible for administering the program.[13]

National Health Service Corps

Congress created the National Health Service Corps in 1970 to help states and communities recruit and place primary care physicians and other health professionals in areas where shortages exist. The sites targeted for the placement of NHSC physicians are usually poor rural and inner-city areas. In 1989 approximately 1,700 physicians, nurses, and others were providing primary care to 2 million people through federal support in the NHSC program, largely in community health centers.[14] The NHSC supplied half the physicians working in community and migrant health centers, as well as nearly one-fourth of Indian Health Service physicians and nearly two-fifths of physicians working in Bureau of Prisons' health facilities.[15]

Initially, the corps relied on a scholarship program that obligated recipients to serve in a shortage area. Beginning in 1981 the scholarship program was dramatically reduced. The rationale for this decrease was that the expected nationwide surplus of physicians would, on its own, prompt providers to practice in underserved areas. By and large, this market strategy did not work. Because of the decline in funding, the number of health professionals newly placed in underserved areas declined from a high of 1,609 in 1985 to 215 in 1989.[16] The NHSC now operates a small scholarship program, a somewhat larger program to recruit providers to serve in return for payment of their educational loans, and demonstration grants to develop state loan repayment programs. Some states on their own are involved in similar programs to encourage health professionals to practice in underserved areas.[17]

The 1980s brought deep cuts to the NHSC program. Fiscal year 1990 funding was $51 million, down by almost two-thirds from the 1980 appropriation. Especially hard hit was the scholarship program, which dropped 96 percent between 1980 and 1990.[18] By contrast, the fiscal 1991 appropriation was $92 million, an important sign that Congress is willing to reverse the previous decade's trends. Since the time lag between the receipt of scholarships and the start of medical practice is so long, there will be a paucity of NHSC providers over the next few years.

The NHSC is administered by the Bureau of Health Care Delivery and Assistance of the Public Health Service. States are not directly responsible for the administration of the program.[19]

Title X Family Planning Programs

Title X of the Public Health Service Act supports family planning clinics, the training of family planning personnel, and the development and dissemination of family planning information.[20] Most title X funds are awarded directly to approximately 4,000 public and nonprofit family planning clinics. Participating clinics offer a range of methods and services, including physical examinations (covering cancer detection and laboratory tests), contraceptive supplies, pregnancy tests, periodic follow-up examinations, referral to other social and medical agencies, and nondirective counseling services.

Although there is no statutorily mandated target population under title X, regulations require that priority be given to persons from low-income families. Clinics must provide services free of charge to persons whose incomes are below the poverty line.

In 1990 federal funding for title X was $136 million.[21] Title X is administered by the Office of Family Planning in the Office of the Assistant Secretary for Health, Department of Health and Human Services. No state matching funds exist for these grants.

Special Supplemental Food Program for Women, Infants, and Children

Although WIC does not directly provide health care, a list of programs designed to improve the health of children and pregnant women would be incomplete without mention of the special supplemental food program for women, infants, and children. The WIC program helps infants, children, and pregnant and breastfeeding women who lack adequate food to meet their nutritional needs.[22] Several studies have shown that participation in WIC increases both prenatal care usage and birth weight.[23] The program, begun in 1972, provides supplemental food, offers nutrition counseling, and refers women and their families to health services. WIC, medicaid, and the maternal and child health program are required to coordinate services. In most states, WIC is one of the largest public health programs for low-income pregnant women and children, but the proportion of eligible women and children served by WIC and the integration of WIC with other health programs vary widely across states.

In 1990 federal funding for the WIC program was $2.1 billion and was expected to serve about 4.5 million people.[24] Because of funding limitations, only about 60 percent of those who financially qualify for WIC services are able to participate.[25]

The Food and Nutrition Service of the U.S. Department of Agriculture awards grants to the state health departments to run their own programs. In addition, public health providers, public welfare agencies, and nonprofit organizations contract with WIC programs to provide health services to WIC-participating mothers and children.

IMPACT OF DELIVERY SYSTEM PROGRAMS

Federally funded delivery system programs are only a small part of the health care system. Nonetheless, where they do operate, these programs have improved access by reducing financial, supply, and organizational barriers and by minimizing cultural and social impediments to use. Moreover, although the data are largely from the 1970s, there is some evidence that these programs improve health status.

Financial Barriers

Subsidized delivery programs play an important role in providing health care to the nation's poor. Approximately 64 percent of the patients in community and migrant health centers and state maternal and child health programs have incomes below the poverty level, and another 31 percent are between 100 and 200 percent of poverty.[26]

About 64 percent of the patients served by C/MHCs are members of minority groups, and 85 percent of those served by migrant health centers are members of minority groups.[27]

Supply Barriers

Community health centers and National Health Service Corps assignments focus on underserved urban and rural areas, where there are serious shortages of health care providers or where providers do not accept medicaid. By design, the NHSC scholarship repayment programs place physicians, and occasionally nurses, practitioners, and midwives, in underserved communities. Neighborhoods served by community health centers increase their use of health services.[28]

Organizational Barriers

Reducing the fragmentation of the health care delivery system and meeting the nonmedical needs of patients are two of the principal goals of public delivery system programs. Without the integration of these two goals, the disadvantaged population faces a patchwork of programs, each at a different location and each with different eligibility requirements. The notion of comprehensive services is that people are more likely to receive the services they need if they can receive them all in one location or with the guidance of a case manager. This is, in marketing vernacular, "one-stop shopping."[29] The Maternal and Child Health Bureau is currently funding demonstration projects of one-stop shopping programs at community and migrant health centers and other sites.[30]

At the Brookings conference, Joycelyn Elders related how she reorganized health department programs. "I decided," she said, "that I did not approve of having poor women make four trips for something that they could get in one. So we aren't going to have any more immunization clinics; we aren't going to have any WIC clinics; we aren't going to have any more 'child health clinics.' We will have just one clinic. Let the mother come in and get the things she needs."

Also at the conference, Aaron Shirley, project director of the Jackson-Hinds Comprehensive Health Center, described the services available at his facility. Besides basic health services, the center provides outreach, a medicaid-eligibility worker on site, dietary counseling, special food vouchers, a high-risk pregnancy management team (consisting of a social worker, a nutritionist, and a health educator), home safety assessments, and well-baby care.

Cultural and Social Barriers

To reach ethnic and racial minority groups, these programs engage in a wide range of outreach services.[31] Examples of innovative approaches are a "mom-mobile" in Indianapolis and Washington, D.C., and the use of celebrity athletes to reach school-aged youth in Detroit. In a project in the Atlanta area funded by the Bureau of Maternal and Child Health, local black Baptist church women have been trained by project staff as "resource mothers" to help pregnant women negotiate the health care and social services systems.[32]

Primary care programs can also provide a wide range of social services that address language, educational, environmental, and other issues that otherwise impede patients' ability to obtain health care services. An example is the women's residential drug treatment program run by the Economic Opportunity Family Health Center in Miami, Florida. This program, which responds to substance abuse among women of childbearing age, offers detoxification and individual and group therapy as well as high-school equivalency preparation, job training and placement, parenting education and counseling, long-term follow-up, and child care on the premises.[33]

Research on Service Expenditures and Health Status

A review of studies done in the mid-1970s suggests that organized delivery systems can affect service use and expenditures as well as improve health status. Important caveats to this conclusion are that the studies are largely based on data at least fifteen years old and are limited in their ability to control for factors that might affect service use and health status.

Community and migrant health center patients appear to have lower use of expensive hospital and other services. For example, a 1970s' study of five cities found that hospital days for such patients were 20 to 25 percent less than those for persons who did not use C/MHCs.[34] In a three-city study of service use, medicaid recipients who were users of community health centers had total medicaid costs

TABLE 6-1. *Federal Appropriations and Expenditures for Selected Health Programs, Fiscal Years 1980–90*
Millions of dollars unless otherwise specified

Year	Maternal and child health block grant	Community/migrant health centers and infant mortality initiative	National Health Service Corps	Total	Medicaid	Medical consumer price index[a]
1980	433	360	154	947	14,000	74.9
1981	455	367	148	970	16,800	82.9
1982	374	319	131	824	17,400	92.5
1983	478	398	104	980	19,000	100.6
1984	399	393	74	866	20,100	106.8
1985	478	427	48	953	22,700	113.5
1986	457	441	58	956	25,000	122.0
1987	497	465	42	1,004	27,400	130.1
1988	527	459	43	1,029	30,500	138.6
1989	554	481	48	1,083	34,600	149.3
1990	554	506	51	1,111	41,100	161.9[b]
Average annual compound rate of growth (percent)	2.5	3.5	−10.5	1.6	11.3	8.0

Sources: Edward R. Klebe, "Appropriations for Selected Health Programs: FY 1980–FY 1990," *CRS Report for Congress,* 90-360 EPW, (Congressional Research Service, 1990); *Budget of the United States Government, Fiscal Year 1992,* pt. 7, table 8.2, p. 7, table 8.2, pt. 7, pp. 79–82; and *Social Security Bulletin,* vol. 53 (November 1990), table M-41, p. 74.
a. Calendar rather than fiscal years.
b. As of June 1990.

of 6–58 percent less than a control group of medicaid recipients who relied on hospitals and private physicians for their usual source of care.[35]

Organized delivery systems also appear to have a positive effect on health status. Compared with users of traditional medicaid services, pregnant women who participated in state outreach or case management programs had babies with higher birth weights.[36] In a nationwide analysis using time-series data and multivariate regression techniques, counties served by health centers had lower infant mortality than those in comparable counties.[37] Similarly, one study attributed a 60 percent decrease in rheumatic fever in areas served by primary care centers to early detection and treatment of streptococcal infections.[38]

ISSUES IN SERVICE DELIVERY PROGRAMS

Making service delivery programs work in the reality of an inner-city neighborhood or in rural areas with few resources is not easy. Programs and providers face serious problems, including low levels of funding, program fragmentation, recruitment and retention of health professionals, and third-party resistance to funding nonmedical services.

Level of Funding

Delivery system programs have three funding problems. First, the aggregate level of expenditures is small, especially compared with the medicaid program (table 6-1). Obviously, small programs can affect only a limited number of people.

Second, because they are discretionary rather than entitlement programs, funding for the maternal and child health block grant, community and migrant health centers, and the National Health Service Corps has been vulnerable to tight budget constraints. For example, appropriations for these programs increased only 1.6 percent a year between 1980 and 1990, not even keeping pace with the medical care inflation rate of 8.0 percent a year. By contrast, medicaid expenditures increased by 11.3 percent a year between 1980 and 1990. Expenditures for discretionary programs increase only when there is a conscious decision to do so; with entitlement programs, increases in the number of recipients and the cost of services alone can automatically lead to higher expenditures.

Third, as noted in chapter 3, the budget rules established by the Budget Enforcement Act of 1990 will make it very difficult to substantially increase appropriations for delivery system programs. For fiscal 1992 and 1993, those programs can be increased only by cutting other domestic programs. For fiscal 1994 and 1995, they can be increased only by cutting military, international, or other domestic discretionary spending. Given the political difficulty of making such cuts, the prospects for large increases in appropriations for programs like community health centers and the maternal and child health block grant seem particularly bleak.

Fragmentation

Although comprehensive care is a common goal of these federal programs, funding and administration are highly fragmented. For example, the programs described in this chapter are under the jurisdictions of different congressional committees and are administered by several branches of the Public Health Service of the Department of Health and Human Services, the Department of Agriculture, and state health departments and local grantees. Furthermore, the medicaid program is administered at the federal level by the Health Care Financing Administration, not the Public Health Service, and at the state level usually by welfare, not health, departments.

Recruitment and Retention of Providers

Delivery system programs, such as community health centers, public health departments, and the National Health Service Corps, find it difficult to recruit and retain doctors and other health care professionals. Providers are often reluctant to choose to practice in C/MHCs or health departments because they are unlikely to offer competitive salaries and benefit packages. Moreover, the service populations and the locations may be perceived as undesirable, and in some inner-city areas crime may also be a problem. At the Brookings conference, Reed Tuckson explained that he had to end evening hours at some Washington, D.C., public health clinics because he could not guarantee the personal safety of the staff.

The recruitment of physicians, as well as the continuity of care, may also may be impeded because of a poor relationship with hospitals. In some cases, C/MHC physicians do not have admitting privileges at the referral hospitals, thus limiting practice opportunities and disrupting the continuity of care. At the conference, Shirley argued that some hospitals are reluctant to grant hospital privileges to C/MHC physicians because hospitals believe that large numbers of poor and minority patients will reduce their ability to compete for privately insured patients. Although many small and struggling rural hospitals are anxious to admit any patients so as to boost their sagging occupancy rates, private urban hospitals are increasingly reluctant to accommodate medicaid deliveries. Too many medicaid deliveries may tarnish the image of the facility and make it less attractive to the "more desirable" middle- and upper-income patients with private insurance.

Constraints on Providing Comprehensive Services

Another stumbling block for improving access to health care for special populations is that funding to cover services beyond just medical services is often not available. Third-party payers, such as private insurers, medicare, and medicaid, are under pressure to keep expenditures down. They are also reluctant to fund social and other support services that do not fit the health insurance model of paying for units of service provided. Many state medicaid programs have historically paid C/MHCs based on the state's extremely low private physician fee schedules, thus not recognizing the much higher overhead costs of C/MHCs or public health departments, which provide many additional services beyond medical care for typically high-risk populations. As direct funding of C/MHCs has declined in real terms, centers have been forced to focus their funds on more narrowly defined medical services. The Omnibus Budget Reconciliation Act of 1989 attempted to alleviate this problem by requiring medicaid programs to pay C/MHCs on a "reasonable cost" basis reflecting their actual costs.

Resistance to comprehensive care is not purely financial. Disapproving attitudes on the part of some providers, policymakers, insurers, and others about nontraditional services for family planning, substance abuse, AIDS, prenatal care, and even dental and mental health contribute to the hesitation to invest in those services. At the conference, Elders noted that the controversy over providing family planning services to teenagers has hampered the expansion of school health programs. In her opinion, opponents of providing family planning services miss this fact: the high teenage birthrate demonstrates that sexual activity already exists and should by openly addressed.

CONCLUSION

Improving access to health services for pregnant women and children, especially those with low incomes, will require more than just providing a financing mechanism like medicaid or private insurance. Financing strategies alone cannot fully address the myriad nonfinancial barriers to care. This is particularly true for such groups as pregnant and parenting teenagers, low-income families, substance-abusing pregnant women, and children with chronic illnesses who face many nonmedical problems affecting their health. Delivery system programs, such as the maternal and child health block grant and community and migrant health centers, aim to increase the supply and to broaden the scope of services available.

The limited research available suggests that community health centers and other delivery system programs have had a positive effect on reducing financial, capacity, organizational, and cultural and social barriers to care. These supply-side programs have had their successes but still face critical problems. Despite positive results, funding for these programs has not kept pace with the need and has not matched the increases in the medicaid program. Because of the emphasis on deficit reduction over the last decade, it has been extremely difficult to obtain budget increases for appropriated as opposed to entitlement programs. Budget constraints have also forced the curtailment of some of the broad-ranging services that are the hallmark of these programs.

CHAPTER SEVEN

Where Do We Go from Here?

The health status of children and pregnant women in the United States is not what it should be. And the health status of some groups, such as African-Americans, is much worse than that of the rest of the population. One reason for poor health outcomes is that many children and pregnant women do not have access to basic health services. Even when coverage is available, such as through the medicaid program, providers may not be available or be willing to provide services. Complicating this basic access problem are many social problems, including poverty, poor nutrition, drugs, crime, substandard housing, and unemployment. Traditional medical approaches are simply too narrow to address this wide array of problems. Moreover, programs that take a broader perspective, such as maternal and child health programs, school-based clinics, and community health centers, are inadequately funded.

At the July 1989 Brookings conference, several strategies were proposed to improve access to health services for pregnant women and children. Analytically, these strategies can be categorized along two dimensions. The first dimension is whether the proposal depends on the public or private sector as the principal financing source. The second is whether the proposal is a financing strategy, like private insurance or medicaid, or whether it is a service delivery strategy, like the maternal and child health program and the community and migrant health centers. In the real world, these approaches are not neatly distinguished; indeed, they are inextricably intertwined.

PUBLIC VERSUS PRIVATE OPTIONS

The key question is whether the public sector, primarily federal and state governments, should provide the funds for expanded services to pregnant women and children, or whether that burden should be borne by the private sector, primarily businesses and their employees.[1] Although the cost to society may be equivalent between the two approaches, the political implications of the two strategies are dramatically different.

Advantages of Public Sector Options

Publicly funded strategies have three advantages. First, it is generally agreed that paying for the health care of the poor is an appropriate government role. Although Americans may disagree over whether this responsibility resides at the federal, state, or local level, both conservatives and liberals believe the public sector has a responsibility to make sure that the poor receive some level of medical care.

Second, public sector programs are also more likely to be designed to meet the needs of the low-income population, some of whom have considerable medical and social needs. Moreover, certain public programs, such as community health centers and the National Health Service Corps, increase the supply of providers by consciously placing them in underserved areas.

Third, a number of programs already exist that can be incrementally expanded. Such programs as medicaid, the maternal and child health program, and community health centers already serve many people who would not otherwise have access to health care. Thus an administrative infrastructure already exists, and programs can be expanded to serve larger numbers of people.

Advantages of Private Sector Options

In contrast, advocates of private sector strategies contend that nongovernmental strategies are preferable. For one thing, with the annual federal budget deficit reaching $362 billion for fiscal 1992, it may not be practical to depend on initiatives that assume large increases in federal spending.[2] State governments are in the same situation. Even if they offer tax breaks to ease the financial burden on small companies, proposals to encourage or mandate private insurance will result in smaller direct or indirect public costs.

A second advantage of private insurance is that it could help integrate the uninsured into the rest of the population. Since health insurance would largely be tied to the workplace, expanded private insurance could strengthen incentives to work. At the same time, private insurance lacks the welfare stigma of medicaid, community health centers, and other public programs that lead some eligible people not to enroll or use services.

Finally, broad middle-class participation in private insurance would help guarantee adequate funding for the uninsured. Private insurance may be freer of the funding problems that plague medicaid and other public programs.

FINANCING VERSUS DELIVERY SYSTEM REFORM OPTIONS

Financing strategies for improving access to health care, such as private insurance and medicaid, make people eligible for a defined set of benefits. Given financial coverage, people use existing delivery systems—including some that are geared to low-income people. Investing primarily in this approach assumes that the barriers to health care are overwhelmingly financial. Thus the goal would be to increase demand for health services by the uninsured by giving them the financial wherewithal necessary to do so.

While delivery system advocates also stress the financial barriers to access, they challenge the notion that an adequate delivery system exists which the poor can use. Delivery system strategies assume that lack of providers, failure to deal with social as well as medical problems, and fragmented care are major barriers to care that must be addressed if access to care is to improve.

Advantages of Financing Reform Options

Financing options have several advantages. First, the number of people covered can be expanded quite quickly. Simply by raising financial eligibility levels for medicaid, more people can become eligible. In its most extreme formulation, handing out medicaid cards can be done rather fast. Financing programs usually do not require the more difficult development of new organizations that is the hallmark of delivery system approaches.

Another advantage of medicaid and private insurance is that they are entitlements. Once people are eligible for services, the government or private insurers are legally responsible to pay for covered medically necessary services. This means that expenditures are more likely to increase with need than they are in directly appropriated programs, such as community health centers and the maternal and child health block grant, whose funding has historically been low and is subject to the annual appropriations process.

Finally, financing strategies are also attractive because, theoretically, they permit people to have a choice of providers. This choice can integrate the poor into a one-class system. Furthermore, a real choice of providers allows for better-quality care because people can "vote with their feet" and change providers.

Advantages of Delivery System Strategies

One advantage of a delivery system strategy is the ability to focus on the particular needs of poor people in general and pregnant women and children in particular. Ideally, delivery system programs are able to treat the whole person and are not concerned about whether a particular service is "medical care." For example, programs designed for the poor can take into account issues of crime, drug abuse, AIDS, poor nutrition, and cultural differences, among others. Services for community outreach, for clinic transportation, and for connecting people with social services are not traditionally part of medical care, but they are services that can make the difference between having some care and being able to improve potentially unhealthy life-styles. The current system of health care for children and pregnant women, particularly those who are poor, is fragmented, resulting in inadequate care. Delivery system strategies make coordination of services a priority.

Delivery system approaches also address the fact that there are few providers in many inner-city and rural areas. The availability of obstetrician-gynecologists has been a particular problem. Therefore, a medicaid or insurance card may not give a person access to services. By placing health care providers in these underserved areas, delivery system programs seek to directly counter this problem. Although that creates a separate system for the poor, advocates of this approach argue that the poor need so many more services that a somewhat separate system, ready and able to meet their complex needs, may be a better way to improve their health.

The Real World: Public and Private, Financing and Delivery

Distinctions between pure types of public and private funding and between financing and delivery strategies are analytically useful, but they mask the complexities of the real world. In practice, these approaches are interdependent. For example, the viability of private health insurance is heavily dependent on its tax deductibility as a business expense, which reduces tax revenues and is as much a cost to the government as direct expenditure for the medicaid program. Moreover, at least for children and pregnant women, the medicaid program is taking on some of the characteristics of delivery system programs by sponsoring outreach, coordinating care, and expanding the range of services. Similarly, delivery system programs, such as community health centers, are increasingly turning to medicaid as a source of revenue for their operations, reserving appropriated funds for persons who are not medicaid eligible. Out in the trenches where services are actually delivered, pure types do not exist and combinations flourish.

FINAL THOUGHTS

At the Brookings conference, Alice Rivlin noted that the roots of the nation's high infant mortality rate and poor child health go far beyond an inadequate health care system and its financing. However, she contended that the complexity of these problems should not paralyze efforts to improve the health care sector. There is no logic to waiting for improvements in education and the economy before we develop mechanisms to improve access to health care.

What kind of health services structure should the United States move toward? The consensus at the conference was that both financing and delivery system approaches play important roles in improving access to health care for many groups of people. But neither approach is adequate alone. There seemed to be agreement that each approach could work better if they could work together.

There is no shortage of proposals that would have a positive impact on access to health services for pregnant women and children. But virtually all of them face enormous barriers to implementation, principally lack of funding. Despite lofty pronouncements by politicians and others about the importance of providing health care to pregnant women and children, funding in both the public and private sectors remains inadequate. To date, Americans have preferred to spend their money on other things. The key question is whether we, as a society, have the political will to reorder our priorities and make the health of future generations a vital concern.

Changes in the Medicaid Eligibility Policy

Although medicaid is the chief health financing program for the low-income population, it covers only about 40 percent of the poor.[1] While medicaid's financial eligibility requirements for pregnant women and young children are more generous than those for other groups, its general financial eligibility ceilings are extremely low—less than 50 percent of the poverty line in most states.[2] As a result, most low-income people do not qualify for benefits. Furthermore, medicaid covers only certain categories of the poor—principally the aged, the blind, the disabled, families with dependent children, and pregnant women. Most states also cover people in those categories who have high medical expenses. Those people who do not fit the categories are simply out of luck, regardless of how serious their health needs are.

Historically, eligibility for medicaid has been tightly linked to receipt of cash welfare assistance, mainly aid to families with dependent children (AFDC) and supplemental security income. Between 1975 and 1986 the proportion of the poor covered by medicaid steadily declined, because states' income eligibility levels for AFDC did not keep pace with inflation.[3] With states either freezing or actually reducing the maximum financial eligibility for AFDC, the welfare income threshold dropped from an average of 71 percent of poverty in 1975 to 48 percent in 1986.[4] The removal of most of the working poor from the AFDC program as a result of the Omnibus Budget Reconciliation Act of 1981 exacerbated this trend.

States, eager to improve the health of low-income families and gain more control over their medicaid programs, joined forces with maternal and child health advocates and successfully lobbied Congress to increase eligibility levels and to break the link between medicaid eligibility and AFDC for young children and pregnant women. While it has expanded eligibility, this approach has created "notch problems"; for example, a pregnant mother will be eligible for medicaid but not her husband, or some children in a family will be eligible because they are below a certain age while others, perhaps only a year older, will not be eligible.

Starting in 1984, Congress began giving states the option, and then requiring them, to cover certain categories of children and pregnant women who did not receive AFDC cash assistance. The Deficit Reduction Act of 1984 required states to cover people who met the financial eligibility requirements for AFDC but who belonged to certain categories that some states did not cover. States had to cover pregnant single women who met state AFDC income and resource requirements even if they had no other children, and pregnant married women who met those requirements if the principal breadwinner in the family was unemployed. Children born after September 30, 1983, up to age 5 were also eligible for coverage.[5] In all cases, coverage was to begin with the verification of the pregnancy.

The Consolidated Omnibus Budget Reconciliation Act of 1985 expanded the coverage provisions so that states must disregard the employment status of the principal breadwinner and provide medicaid coverage to pregnant women in two-parent families who meet AFDC income and asset standards. In other words, the fact that a poor pregnant women is married to a working spouse will no longer prevent medicaid eligibility.[6]

Congress set in motion a series of legislative steps to cut medicaid ties to AFDC with the passage of the Omnibus Budget Reconciliation Act of 1986 (OBRA 86), which permitted states to extend medicaid coverage to pregnant women and, on an incremental basis, to children up to age 5 with family incomes below a state-established level. States could choose an income eligibility level between the AFDC level and 100 percent of the federal poverty level. The imposition of resource (or asset) tests was made optional.[7] That is, OBRA 86 permitted states to forgo scrutinizing the value of the assets of pregnant women, allowing income to be the only criterion for eligibility. Forgoing the assets test was included partly as a way to simplify and, therefore, to speed up the eligibility determination process. Most of the states have chosen to drop the assets test.[8] The states retaining assets tests have raised the limits in order to exclude only those women with relatively high resources.

The Omnibus Budget Reconciliation Act of 1987 (OBRA 87) permitted states to expand the scope of eligibility. It allowed states to accelerate coverage of children aged 5 and under whose income was below the federal poverty line. States could immediately include children under age 2, 3, 4, or 5 (as selected by the state). States also could expand coverage to older children living in poverty, so that by fiscal 1991, states could cover all eligible children under age 8.[9] OBRA 87 also let states provide medicaid eligibility to infants (up to age 1) and pregnant women with incomes up to 185 percent of the federal poverty level. States would be allowed to charge beneficiaries for coverage, although no state has yet imposed a premium.[10]

With passage of the Medicare Catastrophic Coverage Act of 1988 (MCCA), states were required to phase in coverage of pregnant women and infants with incomes up to 100 percent of the poverty line.[11] Although the medicare-related portions of the MCCA were repealed in December 1989, Congress left the medicaid portions of the law in place.

In the Omnibus Budget Reconciliation Act of 1989 (OBRA 89), Congress expanded mandatory medicaid eligibility to pregnant women in families with incomes up to 133 percent of the poverty level and children to age 6 in families up to the poverty level. OBRA 89 also permitted, but did not mandate, states to cover children up to age 8 whose family income is under the federal poverty level.

The Omnibus Budget Reconciliation Act of 1990 significantly expanded medicaid eligibility for children, although only minor changes were made for pregnant women. On a phased-in basis, states must provide medicaid eligibility for children in families below 100 percent of the poverty line up to age 19. Further, states must provide medicaid eligibility for pregnant women through the sixtieth postpartum day and for infants through the first year of life.

Medicaid Coverage of Children and Pregnant Women as of January 1991

Over the last several years, Congress has liberalized medicaid eligibility for children and pregnant women.[1] As noted, the Omnibus Budget Reconciliation Act of 1989 mandated that all states, beginning April 1, 1990, cover children to age 6 who live below the federal poverty level and pregnant women below 133 percent of the poverty level. As of January 1991, twenty-four states had gone beyond this mandated expansion of eligibility (table B-1). Of those, eighteen were at the highest level permitted—185 percent. The Omnibus Budget Reconciliation Act of 1990 mandated states to phase in coverage of children to age 19 living below the poverty line. Currently, sixteen states provide medicaid eligibility to all children between ages 6 and 9 living at or below 100 percent of the poverty level.

Several states have also expanded coverage for pregnant women and children beyond medicaid through state-funded programs. California covers pregnant women with incomes up to 200 percent of the federal poverty level. The Maine Health Program covers children up to age 18 living at or below 125 percent of the federal poverty level with no assets test. The Maine Program also covers persons age 18 and older living at up to 95 percent of the federal poverty level with an asset limit of $20,000. Vermont covers children under age 7 who live at or below 225 percent of the federal poverty level and pregnant women at or below 200 percent. Washington state, effective January 1, 1991, covers children to age 18 living at up to 100 percent of the federal poverty level. Wisconsin currently covers children to age 6 living at or below 155 percent of the federal poverty level.

States continue to take advantage of congressional options to simplify the medicaid eligibility process. Fully forty-six states no longer review clients' assets when determining eligibility for pregnant women and children (table B-2). As of January 1991, all states provide continuous medicaid eligibility for pregnant women through sixty days postpartum regardless of fluctuations in income, as required by the Omnibus Budget Reconciliation Act of 1990. A total of twenty-six states grant temporary eligibility to pregnant women while their formal applications are completed and reviewed.

States are also working to improve the health status of low-income pregnant women and infants by expanding the types of prenatal care services that they will cover. As of January 1991, a total of thirty-three states had implemented new programs of enhanced prenatal care, adding comprehensive nonmedical and medical benefits financed through medicaid (table B-3).

TABLE B-1. *Medicaid Coverage Options for Children and Pregnant Women, Summary Status, Omnibus Budget Reconciliation Act, 1986, 1987, 1989*

State	Pregnant women and infants (percent of poverty)[a]	Children aged 6 to 8 (percent of poverty)	Effective date of original expansion
Alabama			July 1988
Alaska			January 1989
Arizona	140	100	January 1988
Arkansas		100	April 1987
California	185	100	July 1989
Colorado			July 1989
Connecticut	185		April 1988
Delaware		100	January 1988
District of Columbia	185	100	April 1987
Florida	150	100	October 1987
Georgia			January 1989
Hawaii	185	100	January 1989
Idaho			January 1989
Illinois			July 1988
Indiana			July 1988
Iowa	185	100	January 1989
Kansas	150		July 1988
Kentucky	185		October 1987
Louisiana		100	January 1989
Maine	185	100	October 1988
Maryland	185		July 1987
Massachusetts	185		July 1987
Michigan	185		January 1988
Minnesota	185	100	July 1988
Mississippi	185		October 1987
Missouri			January 1988
Montana		100	July 1989
Nebraska			July 1988
Nevada			July 1989
New Hampshire			July 1989
New Jersey			July 1987
New Mexico			January 1988
New York	185		January 1990
North Carolina	185	100	October 1987
North Dakota			July 1989

TABLE B-1 *(continued)*

State	Pregnant women and infants (percent of poverty)[a]	Children aged 6 to 8 (percent of poverty)	Effective date of original expansion
Ohio			January 1989
Oklahoma			January 1988
Oregon			November 1987
Pennsylvania			April 1988
Rhode Island	185		April 1987
South Carolina	185		October 1987
South Dakota			July 1988
Tennessee	150		July 1987
Texas			September 1988
Utah			January 1989
Vermont	185	100	October 1987
Virginia			July 1988
Washington	185	100	July 1987
West Virginia	150	100	July 1987
Wisconsin	155		April 1988
Wyoming			October 1988
Number	24	16	

Source: National Governors' Association "State Coverage of Pregnant Women and Children, January 1991," Washington, 1991.

a. Effective April 1, 1990, states must cover pregnant women below 133 percent of the federal poverty level and children to age 6 below the poverty level. For those states that have expanded coverage beyond the mandated 133 percent, this column indicates the percentage of poverty adopted by the state.

TABLE B-2 *Strategies to Streamline Eligibility of Children and Pregnant Women, January 1991*

State	Dropped assets test	Continuous eligibility[a]	Presumptive eligibility	Outstationing eligibility workers	Shortened application	Expedited eligibility
Alabama	X	X	X	X	X	
Alaska	X	X				X
Arizona	X	X				X
Arkansas	X	X	X	X	X	
California		X		X		
Colorado	X	X	X		X	
Connecticut	X	X				
Delaware	X	X		X	X	X
District of Columbia	X	X				
Florida	X	X	X	X	X	
Georgia	X	X		X	X	X
Hawaii	X	X	X			
Idaho	X	X	X			
Illinois		X	X			
Indiana	X	X	X			
Iowa		X	X	X		
Kansas	X	X				X
Kentucky	X	X		X	X	
Louisiana	X	X	X	X	X	
Maine	X	X	X			
Maryland	X	X	X	X[b]	X	
Massachusetts	X	X	X		X	
Michigan	X	X		X[b]	X	
Minnesota	X	X			X	X
Mississippi	X	X		X		
Missouri	X	X	X	X		
Montana	X	X	X			
Nebraska	X	X	X			
Nevada	X	X				
New Hampshire	X	X		X		
New Jersey	X	X	X		X	
New Mexico	X	X	X	X[b]	X	
New York	X	X	X		X	

TABLE B-2 *(continued)*

State	Dropped assets test	Continuous eligibility[a]	Presumptive eligibility	Outstationing eligibility workers	Shortened application	Expedited eligibility
North Carolina	X	X	X	X	X	
North Dakota		X				
Ohio	X	X		X[b]	X	X
Oklahoma	X	X	X		X	
Oregon	X	X			X	X
Pennsylvania	X	X	X			
Rhode Island	X	X				
South Carolina	X	X		X	X	
South Dakota	X	X			X	
Tennessee	X	X	X	X		
Texas		X	X	X	X	
Utah	X	X	X	X		
Vermont	X	X		X[b]	X	X
Virginia	X	X		X	X	X
Washington	X	X			X	X
West Virginia	X	X		X	X	X
Wisconsin	X	X	X		X	X
Wyoming	X	X				
Number	46	51	26	24	27	13

Source: See table B-1.

a. The Omnibus Budget Reconciliation Act of 1990 required all states to provide continuous eligibility to pregnant women and infants, effective January 1, 1991.

b. Instead of placing eligibility workers at health care sites, these states are training provider staff in these settings to administer medicaid applications to potentially eligible clients.

TABLE B-3. *Medicaid Enhanced Prenatal Care Services, January 1991*

State	Care coordination/case management	Risk assessment	Nutritional counseling	Health education	Psychosocial counseling	Home visiting	Transport
Alabama	X	X				X	
Alaska	X	X	X			X	
Arizona							
Arkansas	X	X	X	X	X	X	
California	X	X	X	X	X	X[a]	
Colorado							
Connecticut		X		X		X	
Delaware	X	X	X	X	X	X	
District of Columbia							
Florida							
Georgia	X	X		X[a]		X[a]	
Hawaii	X	X	X	X			
Idaho	X	X	X		X	X	
Illinois	X	X					
Indiana							
Iowa	X	X	X	X	X		
Kansas		X	X	X		X	
Kentucky							
Louisiana	X	X					
Maine							
Maryland	X	X	X	X	X	X	
Massachusetts	X	X	X	X	X		
Michigan	X	X	X	X	X	X	X
Minnesota	X	X	X	X	X	X	
Mississippi	X	X	X	X	X	X	X
Missouri	X	X					
Montana							
Nebraska							
Nevada	X	X	X	X	X	X	
New Hampshire	X	X	X	X	X	X	
New Jersey	X	X	X	X	X	X	
New Mexico	X						
New York	X	X	X	X	X	X	
North Carolina	X	X		X		X	
North Dakota							

TABLE B-3 *(continued)*

State	Care coordination/ case management	Risk assess- ment	Nutri- tional counseling	Health education	Psychosocial counseling	Home visiting	Trans- port
Ohio	X	X	X	X	X	X	
Oklahoma							
Oregon	X	X	X	X		X	
Pennsylvania	X	X	X	X	X	X	
Rhode Island							
South Carolina	X	X	X	X	X	X	
South Dakota							
Tennessee	X	X				X	
Texas							
Utah	X	X	X	X	X	X	
Vermont	X					X	X
Virginia	X	X	X	X		X	
Washington	X	X	X	X	X	X	X
West Virginia	X	X	X	X			
Wisconsin							
Wyoming							
Number	33	33	25	26	19	27	4

Source: See table B-1.
a. Future implementation date.

Notes

CHAPTER ONE

1. United Nations, *Demographic Yearbook*, 40th issue (New York, 1990), table 15, pp. 396–403.

2. U.S. National Center for Health Statistics (NCHS), "Advance Report of Final Mortality Statistics, 1987," *Monthly Vital Statistics Report*, vol. 38, no. 5 supp. (September 26, 1989), table E, p. 8.

3. NCHS, *Health, United States, 1989* (U.S. Department of Health and Human Services [DHHS], 1990), p. 96.

4. Ibid., table 7, p. 97.

5. George H. W. Bush, "Address before a Joint Session of the Congress on the State of the Union, January 29, 1991," *Weekly Compilation of Presidential Documents*, vol. 27 (February 4, 1991), p. 93.

6. *Budget of the United States Government, Fiscal Year 1992*, pt.2, pp. 21–34.

7. Committee for Economic Development, *Children in Need: Investment Strategies for the Educationally Disadvantaged* (New York, 1987); National Commission to Prevent Infant Mortality, *Death before Life: The Tragedy of Infant Mortality* (Washington, 1988); Ford Foundation, *The Common Good: Social Welfare and the American Future* (New York, 1989); Health Policy Agenda for the American People, *The Health Policy Agenda for the American People* (Chicago: American Medical Association, 1987); National Leadership Commission on Health Care, *For the Health of a Nation* (Ann Arbor, Mich.: Health Administration Press Perspectives, 1989); Birt Harvey, "A Proposal to Provide Health Insurance to All Children and All Pregnant Women," *New England Journal of Medicine*, vol. 323 (October 25, 1990), pp. 1216–20; and U.S. Bipartisan Commission on Comprehensive Health Care (Pepper Commission), *A Call For Action: Final Report* (Washington: Government Printing Office, September 1990).

8. NCHS, *Vital Statistics of the United States, 1988*, vol. 2: *Mortality* (DHHS, 1990), pt. B, table 8-2, p. 87.

9. NCHS, *Health, United States, 1989*, table 15, p. 107.

10. Ibid., p. 116; NCHS, *Vital Statistics of the United States, 1987*, vol. 2: *Mortality* (DHHS, 1990), pt. A, table 2-10, pp. 10–11; and NCHS, *Vital Statistics of the United States, 1988*, vol. 2: *Mortality*, pt. B, table 8-2, p. 87.

11. Institute of Medicine, *Preventing Low Birthweight* (Washington: National Academy Press, 1985), p. 27.

12. Stephen Chaikund and Hope Corman, "The Special Education Costs of Low Birthweight," Working Paper 3461 (Cambridge, Mass.: National Bureau of Economic Research [NBER], October 1990).

13. J. Tyson and others, "Prenatal Care Evaluation and Cohort Analyses," *Pediatrics*, vol. 85 (February 1990), pp. 195–204.

14. NCHS, "Advance Report of Final Natality Statistics, 1988," *Monthly Vital Statistics Report*, vol. 39, no. 4 supp. (August 15, 1990), p. 41.

15. Richard G. Frank and others, "Updated Estimates of the Impact of Prenatal Care on Birthweight Outcomes by Race," Working Paper 3624 (NBER, 1991). Selection bias may result in underestimates of the effects of prenatal care. Theodore Joyce, "Self-Selection, Prenatal Care, and Birthweight among Blacks, Whites and Hispanics in New York City," Working Paper 3549 (NBER, December 1990).

16. Alan Guttmacher Institute, *Blessed Events and the Bottom Line: Financing Maternity Care in the United States* (New York, 1987), p. 14.

17. Institute of Medicine, *Preventing Low Birthweight*, p. 232.

18. Robin D. Gorsky and John P. Colby, Jr., "The Cost Effectiveness of Prenatal Care in Reducing Low Birth Weight in New Hampshire," *Health Services Research*, vol. 24 (December 1989), pp. 583–98.

19. American Academy of Pediatrics, *Child Health Financing Report* (Evanston, Ill., Spring 1984), p. 4.

20. Mathematica Policy Research, Inc., *The Savings in Medicaid Costs for Newborns and Their Mothers from Prenatal Participation in the WIC Program* (U.S. Department of Agriculture, 1990), vol. 1, p. 46.

21. NCHS, *Health, United States, 1989*, table 121, p. 250.

22. Alan Guttmacher Institute, *Blessed Events and the Bottom Line*, pp. 21, 43.

23. Congressional Research Service, *Medicaid Source Book: Background Data and Analysis*, Committee Print, prepared for the Subcommittee on Health and Environment of the House Committee on Energy and Commerce (GPO, November 1988), pp. 275, 280.

24. Robert Wood Johnson Foundation, *Access to Health Care in the United States: Results of 1986 Survey*, Special Report, no. 2 (Princeton, N.J., 1987).

25. Howard E. Freeman and others, "Uninsured Working-Age Adults: Characteristics and Consequences," *Health Services Research*, vol. 24 (February 1990), p. 819.

26. Paula Braverman and others, "Average Outcomes of Lack of Health Insurance among Newborns in an Eight County Area of California, 1982–1986," *New England Journal of Medicine*, vol. 321 (August 24, 1989), pp. 508–13.

CHAPTER TWO

1. William Ryan, *Blaming the Victim* (Vintage Books, 1971).

2. Center on Budget and Policy Priorities, *WIC Briefing* (Washington, July 23, 1990).

3. U.S. National Center for Health Statistics (NCHS), *Health, United States, 1989* (U.S. Department of Health and Human Services [DHHS], 1990), table 53, p. 165.

4. R. S. Hopkins, L. E. Tyler, and B. K. Mortensen, "Effects of Maternal Cigarette Smoking on Birth Weight and Preterm Birth—Ohio, 1989," *Morbidity and Mortality Weekly Report*, vol. 39 (September 28, 1990), pp. 662–64.

5. Joel C. Kleinman and others, "The Effects of Maternal Smoking on Fetal and Infant Mortality," *American Journal of Epidemiology*, vol. 27 (February, 1988), pp. 274–82.

6. Bengt Haglund and others, "Cigarette Smoking as a Risk Factor for Sudden Infant Death Syndrome: A Population-Based Study," *American Journal of Public Health*, vol. 80 (January 1990), pp. 29–32.

7. National Institute on Drug Abuse, "NIDA Capsules: Highlights of the

1988 National Household Survey on Drug Abuse," U.S. Department of Health and Human Services, Rockville, Md., August 1989, p. 2.

8. National Association for Perinatal Addiction Research and Education, news release, August 28, 1988, pp. 1–2.

9. Ira J. Chasnoff and others, "The Prevalence of Illicit Drug or Alcohol Use during Pregnancy and Discrepancies in Mandatory Reporting in Pinellas County, Florida," *New England Journal of Medicine*, vol. 322 (April 26, 1990), pp. 1202–06.

10. Gilberto F. Chavez and others, "Maternal Cocaine Use during Early Pregnancy as a Risk Factor for Congenital Urogenital Anomalies," *Journal of the American Medical Association*, vol. 262 (August 11, 1989), pp. 795–98.

11. U.S. General Accounting Office (GAO), *Drug Exposed Infants: A Generation at Risk*, GAO/HRD-90-138 (June 1990), p. 1.

12. Ibid., p. 6.

13. Ibid., p. 7.

14. Douglas J. Besharov, "Crack Babies: The Worst Threat Is Mom Herself," *Washington Post*, August 6, 1989, p. B4.

15. GAO, *Drug Exposed Infants*, pp. 7–8; and Marilyn Littlejohn and Kenneth Thomas, *Cocaine/Crack Babies: Health Problems, Treatment and Prevention*, Congressional Research Service 89-601 SPR (Library of Congress, October 30, 1989), pp. 7–9.

16. Rodney Hoff and others, "Seroprevalence of Human Immunodeficiency Virus among Childbearing Women," *New England Journal of Medicine*, vol. 318 (March 3, 1988), pp. 527–29.

17. Susan Y. Chu and others, "Impact of the Human Immunodeficiency Virus Epidemic on Mortality in Women of Reproductive Age, United States," *Journal of the American Medical Association*, vol. 264 (July 11, 1990), pp. 225–29.

18. Michael K. Lindsay and others, "Routine Antepartum Human Immunodeficiency Virus Infection Screening in an Inner-City Population," *Obstetrics and Gynecology*, vol. 74 (September 1989), pp. 289–94.

19. Chu and others, "Impact of the Human Immunodeficiency Virus Epidemic," pp. 225–29.

20. Amy Goldstein, "AIDS Cases Rising in D.C. Women," *Washington Post*, June 8, 1991, pp. A1, A10.

21. Stephane Blanche and others, "A Prospective Study of Infants Born to Women Seropositive for Human Immunodeficiency Virus Type 1," *New England Journal of Medicine*, vol. 320 (June 22, 1989), pp. 1643–48.

22. Lindsay and others, "Routine Antepartum Human Immunodeficiency Virus," pp. 289–94.

23. Centers for Disease Control, *HIV/AIDS Surveillance Report* (Washington, July 1990), p. 12.

24. Hoff and others, "Seroprevalence of Human Immunodeficiency Virus," pp. 527–29.

25. Gwen Scott and others, "Survival in Children with Perinatally-Acquired HIV Infection, Type 1," *New England Journal of Medicine*, vol. 321 (December 28, 1989), p. 1791.

26. Ann Sunderland and others, "Influence of HIV Infection on Pregnancy Decisions," abstract, International AIDS Conference, 1988.

27. Alan Guttmacher Institute, *Blessed Events and the Bottom Line: Financing Maternity Care in the United States* (New York, 1987), pp. 6–7.

28. Congressional Budget Office, *Sources of Support for Adolescent Mothers* (September 1990), p. xvii.
29. NCHS, "Advance Report of Final Natality Statistics, 1988," *Monthly Vital Statistics Report*, vol. 39, no. 4 supp. (August 15, 1990), pp. 1–5.
30. Ibid., pp. 1–5.
31. Ibid., p. 9.
32. Ibid., p. 7.
33. Alan Guttmacher Institute, *Blessed Events and the Bottom Line*, p. 15.
34. Carol J. R. Hogue and Roy Yip, "Preterm Delivery: Can We Lower the Black Infant's First Hurdle?" *Journal of the American Medical Association*, vol. 262 (July 28, 1989), pp. 548–50.
35. NCHS, *Vital Statistics of the United States, 1988*, vol. 1: *Natality, Public Health Service* (DHHS, 1990), sec. 1, table 1-86, p. 255.

CHAPTER THREE

1. Congressional Budget Office, *The Economic and Budget Outlook: An Update* (1991), Summary, table 4, p. xiv.
2. Congressional Budget Office, *The Economic and Budget Outlook, Fiscal Years 1990–1994* (January 1989); Charles L. Schultze, "Of Wolves, Termites, and Pussycats, or, Why We Should Worry about the Budget Deficit," *Brookings Review*, vol. 7 (Summer 1989), pp. 26–33; and Edward M. Gramlich, "Budget Deficits and National Savings: Are Politicians Exogenous?" *Journal of Economic Perspectives*, vol. 3 (Spring 1989), pp. 23–36.
3. For a detailed description of the new budget process and the budget outlook, see Congressional Budget Office, *The Economic and Budget Outlook, Fiscal Years 1992–1996* (1991), pp. 43–78.
4. Robert J. Blendon and Karen Donelan, "The Public and the Emerging Debate over National Health Insurance," *New England Journal of Medicine*, vol. 323 (July 19, 1990), pp. 208–12.
5. Gary F. Burtless, *A Future of Lousy Jobs? The Changing Structure of U.S. Wages* (Brookings, 1990).
6. As Representative Thomas Tauke put it at the conference, "How is it that we spend so much of our GNP on health care in relation to other countries, and when we have this rapidly growing federal commitment, how is it that we aren't making more progress?"

CHAPTER FOUR

1. Alan Guttmacher Institute, *Blessed Events and the Bottom Line: Financing Maternity Care in the United States* (New York, 1987), p. 29.
2. Health Care Financing Administration, "A Statistical Report on Medicaid: Title XIX of the Social Security Act," Baltimore, Md., 1990, table 2, p. 8.
3. U.S. General Accounting Office, *Prenatal Care: Early Success in Enrolling Women Made Eligible by Medicaid Expansions* (1991).
4. Robert J. Blendon and others, "Uncompensated Care by Hospitals or Public Insurance for the Poor," *New England Journal of Medicine*, vol. 414 (May 1, 1986), pp. 1160–63.
5. Robert J. Blendon and others, "Access to Medical Care for Black and

White Americans," *Journal of the American Medical Association*, vol. 261 (January 13, 1989), pp. 278–81.

6. Charles R. Link and others, "Access to Medical Care under Medicaid: Differentials by Race," *Journal of Health Politics, Policy and Law*, vol. 7 (Summer 1982), pp. 345–65.

7. Linda A. Levey and others, "Health Care of Poverty and Nonpoverty Children in Iowa," *American Journal of Public Health*, vol. 76 (August 1986), pp. 1000–03.

8. Alice M. Rivlin and Joshua M. Wiener, with Raymond J. Hanley and Denise A. Spence, *Caring for the Disabled Elderly: Who Will Pay?* (Brookings, 1988), pp. 163–64.

9. John Holahan and Sheila Zedlewski, "Insuring Low-Income Americans through Medicaid Expansion: A Summary of Findings," Working Paper 3836-03 (Washington: Urban Institute, February 1990).

10. John Holahan and Sheila Zedlewski, "Expanding Medicaid to Cover Uninsured Americans," *Health Affairs*, vol. 10 (Spring 1991), pp. 45–61.

11. Although it is not often factored into the decisionmaking process, states with high federal medicaid match-rates derive significant economic stimulus from increased medicaid spending. See, for example, letter from Daniel K. Lee, director of economics, Center for Policy Research and Planning, Mississippi Institutions of Higher Learning, to James C. Lowery, Division of Medicaid, State of Mississippi, December 21, 1988.

12. National Governors' Association, "State Coverage of Pregnant Women and Children, January 1991," Washington, 1991, table 6.

13. Ibid., table 5.

14. Ibid., table 5.

15. Ibid., table 5.

16. U. S. General Accounting Office, *Home Visiting: A Promising Early Intervention Strategy for At-Risk Families*, GAO/HRD-90-83 (July 1990).

17. See also James W. Fossett and others, "Medicaid Patients' Access to Office-Based Obstetricians," University of Chicago, May 1989; Janet D. Perloff, Phillip R. Kletke, and Kathryn M. Neckerman, "Physicians' Decision to Limit Medicaid Participation: Determinants and Policy Implications," *Journal of Health Politics, Policy and Law*, vol. 12 (Summer 1987), pp. 221–35; and James W. Fossett and others, "Medicaid in the Inner City: The Case of Maternity Care in Chicago," *Milbank Quarterly*, vol. 88, no. 1 (1990), pp. 111–41.

18. Deborah Lewis-Idema, *Increasing Provider Participation*, State Policy Reports, Health Studies, Strategies for Improving Perinatal Programs (Washington: National Governors' Association, 1988), table 2, p. 4.

19. Beth K. Yudkowsky and others, "Pediatrician Participation in Medicaid, 1978–1989," paper presented at the American Public Health Association, 118th annual meeting, October 3, 1990.

20. American College of Obstetricians and Gynecologists, *Professional Liability and Its Effects: Report of a 1987 Survey of ACOG's Membership* (Washington, March 1988), p. 11.

21. Institute of Medicine, *Medical Professional Liability and the Delivery of Obstetrical Care* (Washington: National Academy Press, 1989), vol. 1, p. 2.

22. American College of Obstetricians and Gynecologists, *Professional Liability and Its Effects*, p. 22.

23. Institute of Medicine, *Medical Professional Liability*, vol. 1, p. 7.

24. R. A. Rosenblatt and others, "Why Do Physicians Stop Practicing Ob-

stetrics? The Impact of Malpractice Claims," *Obstetrics and Gynecology*, vol. 76 (August 1990), pp. 245–50.

25. For a review of this literature, see Lewis-Idema, *Increasing Provider Participation*, pp. 27–28.

26. Health Insurance Association of America, *The Cost of Maternity Care and Childbirth in the United States, 1989*, Research Bulletin (Washington, December 1989), table 1, p. 5; and American College of Obstetricians and Gynecologists, "Medicaid Reimbursement for Obstetric Care Specialists by State," unpublished data, May 1990. For another analysis of how medicaid physician payment rates compare with medicare and private payment rates, see Anne Schwartz, David C. Colby, and Anne Lenhard Reisinger, "Variations in Medicaid Physician Fees," *Health Affairs*, vol. 10 (Spring 1991), pp. 131–39.

27. Lewis-Idema, *Increasing Provider Participation*, table 4, p. 7.

28. Mark Schlesinger and Karl Kronebusch, "The Failure of Prenatal Care Policy for the Poor," *Health Affairs*, vol. 9 (Winter 1990), pp. 91–111.

29. President's Commission for the Study of Ethical Problems in Medicine and Biomedical and Behavioral Research, *Securing Access to Health Care: The Ethical Implications of Differences in Availability of Health Services*, vol. 1: *Report* (Government Printing Office, March 1983), pp. 83–86; and Janet B. Mitchell and Rachel Schuman, "Access to Private Obstetrics/Gynecology Services under Medicaid," *Medical Care*, vol. 22 (November 1984), pp. 1026–37.

CHAPTER FIVE

1. Employee Benefit Research Institute (EBRI), "Update: Americans without Health Insurance," *EBRI Issue Brief*, no. 104 (July 1990), table 1, p. 3.

2. Ibid., p. 13.

3. Alan Guttmacher Institute, *Blessed Events and the Bottom Line: Financing Maternity Care in the United States* (New York, 1987), p. 21.

4. EBRI, "Update," table 1, p. 3. The percentage of the population that is without health insurance at some period is much larger than the percentage at any point in time. For example, using the National Medical Expenditure Survey, Short estimated that 22.4 percent of the nonelderly population were uninsured at some time during 1987, but fewer—10.4 percent—were uninsured for the entire year. Pamela Farley Short, *Estimates of the Uninsured Population, Calendar Year 1987*, National Medical Expenditure Survey, Data Summary 2, DHHS (PHS) 90-3469 (Rockville, Md.: Public Health Service, Agency for Health Policy Research, 1990), table 1, p. 5.

5. EBRI, "Update," p. 5.

6. Ibid., p. 5.

7. Mark B. Wenneker, Joel S. Weissman, and Arnold M. Epstein, "The Association of Payer with Utilization of Cardiac Procedures in Massachusetts," *Journal of the American Medical Association*, vol. 264 (September 12, 1990), pp. 1255–95; and Jack Hadley, Earl P. Steinberg, and Judith Feder, "Comparison of Uninsured and Privately Insured Hospital Patients," *Journal of the American Medical Association*, vol. 265 (January 16, 1991), pp. 374–79.

8. Alan C. Monheit and Pamela Farley Short, "Mandating Health Coverage for Working Americans," *Health Affairs*, vol. 8 (Winter 1989), table 2, p. 29.

9. Charles P. Hall, Jr., and John M. Kuder, *Small Business and Health Care: Results of a Survey* (Washington: NFIB Foundation, 1990), table 8.4, p. 61.

10. Jeanne Sadler, "States Test Bare-Bones Health Insurance," *Wall Street Journal*, July 19, 1990, pp. B1, B2.

11. U.S. Bipartisan Commission on Comprehensive Health Care, *A Call for Action, Final Report* (Government Printing Office, 1990); National Leadership Commission on Health Care, *For the Health of a Nation: A Shared Responsibility* (Ann Arbor, Mich.: Health Administrative Press Perspectives, 1989); and American Medical Association, *Health Access America* (Chicago, 1990).

12. Emily Friedman, "Health Insurance in Hawaii: Paradise Lost or Found," *Business and Health*, vol. 8 (June 1990), pp. 52–59.

13. Jack Hoadley and Judith Miller Jones, "Expanding Access to Health Care in the States: Experimenting with Mandates in Hawaii and Massachusetts," Issue Brief 555 (Washington: George Washington University National Health Policy Forum, 1990).

14. Dan E. Beauchamp and Ronald L. Rouse, "Universal New York Health Care: A Single Payer Strategy Linking Cost Control and Universal Access," *New England Journal of Medicine*, vol. 223 (September 6, 1990), pp. 640–44.

15. For more detailed descriptions of the proposal by the American Academy of Pediatrics, see Birt Harvey, "A Proposal to Provide Health Insurance to All Children and All Pregnant Women," *New England Journal of Medicine*, vol. 323 (October 25, 1990), pp. 1216–20; and American Academy of Pediatrics, "Children First: A Legislative Proposal" (Washington, n.d.).

16. Howard F. Freeman and others, "Uninsured Working Age Adults: Characteristics and Consequences," *Health Services Research*, vol. 24 (February 1990), table 3, p. 819.

17. Lawrence Lewin at the Brookings conference.

18. Gail R. Wilensky, "The 'Pay or Play' Insurance Gamble: Massachusetts' Plan for Universal Health Coverage," House Wednesday Group, Washington, 1988, p. 8.

19. EBRI, "Update," p. 10.

20. Ibid., p. 10.

21. Hall and Kuder, *Small Business and Health Care*, table 7.24, p. 53.

22. Gail R. Wilensky, "The Real Price of Mandating Health Benefits," *Business and Health*, vol. 7 (March 1989), pp. 32–35.

23. *Minimum Health Benefits for All Workers*, Hearings before the Subcommittee on Health and Environment of the House Committee on Energy and Commerce, 100 Cong. 2 sess. (GPO, 1988), p. 106; cited in Eugene Steuerle, "Mandating Employer Provision of Health Insurance," American Association of Retired Persons' Public Policy Institute, Washington, May 1990, p. 23.

24. Hall and Kuder, *Small Business and Health Care*, table 8.3, p. 60.

25. Bipartisan Commission on Comprehensive Health Care, *Call for Action*, p. 67.

26. Karen Davis, "The Economic Impact of Employer Minimum Health Insurance Coverage," testimony before the Senate Committee on Labor and Human Resources, Washington, November 4, 1987.

27. Davis, "Economic Impact of Employer Minimum Health Insurance Coverage."

28. Monheit and Short, "Mandating Health Coverage," p. 35.

29. Joshua M. Wiener, "Taking Care of the Uninsured," in Barry P. Bosworth and others, *Critical Choices: What the President Should Know about the Economy and Foreign Policy* (Brookings, 1989), p. 129.

30. Office of National Cost Estimates, "National Health Expenditures," *Health Care Financing Review*, vol. 11 (Summer 1990), table 13, p. 24.

31. Wilensky, "The 'Pay or Play' Insurance Gamble."

32. Beauchamp and Rouse, "Single-Payer Strategy," pp. 640–44.

33. Mark V. Nadel, "Health Insurance: Availability and Adequacy for Small Businesses," testimony before the Subcommittee on Antitrust, Monopolies and Business Rights of the Senate Committee on the Judiciary, June 5, 1990.

34. U.S. General Accounting Office (GAO), *Health Insurance: Cost Increases Lead to Coverage Limitation and Cost Shifting*, GAO/HRD-90-68 (May 1990), pp. 26–30.

35. Glenn Kramon, "Medical Insurers Vary Fees to Aid Healthier People," *New York Times*, March 24, 1991, p. A1.

36. In addition, some larger firms are resorting to self-insurance so that they can cap payments for the treatment of AIDS. Albert B. Crenshaw, "Employers Try to Cut AIDS Costs," *Washington Post*, January 6, 1991, p. H11.

37. GAO, *Health Insurance*, p. 29; and Bipartisan Commission on Comprehensive Health Care, *Call for Action*, p. 27.

38. Gail R. Wilensky, "Filling the Gaps in Health Insurance: Impact on Competition," *Health Affairs*, vol. 7 (Summer 1988), pp. 133–49.

39. Jack Hoadley and Judith Miller Jones, "Making the Insurance Marketplace Work for Small Employers," Issue Brief 516 (Washington: George Washington University National Health Policy Forum, 1989).

40. Health Insurance Association of America, "HIAA Small Employer Reforms," Washington, 1991.

CHAPTER SIX

1. Overall, 81 percent of privately insured women began care in the first three months of their pregnancy and made nine or more visits for care, compared with only 36 percent of women with medicaid coverage and 32 percent of women with no health insurance. U.S. General Accounting Office, *Prenatal Care: Medicaid Recipients and Uninsured Women Obtain Insufficient Care*, GAO/HRD 87-137 (1987). In a study of the importance of the payer in the utilization of in-hospital cardiac procedures, Wenneker and others found that privately insured patients were much more likely to receive certain procedures than were either medicaid patients or the uninsured. The experience of the medicaid patients was similar to that of the uninsured. Mark B. Wenneker, Joel S. Weissman, and Arnold M. Epstein, "The Association of Payer with Utilization of Cardiac Procedures in Massachusetts," *Journal of the American Medical Association*, vol. 264 (September 12, 1990), pp. 1255–60.

2. Joyce M. Piper, Wayne A. Ray, and Marie R. Griffin, "Effects of Medicaid Eligibility Expansion on Prenatal Care and Pregnancy Outcomes in Tennessee," *Journal of the American Medical Association*, vol. 264 (November 7, 1990), pp. 2219–23.

3. Institute of Medicine, *Prenatal Care: Reaching Mothers, Reaching Infants* (Washington: National Academy Press, 1988), pp. 4–7.

4. Gail R. Wilensky, "Filling the Gaps in Health Insurance: Impact on Competition," *Health Affairs*, vol. 7 (Summer 1988), p. 141.

5. Louise Russell, "Proposed: A Comprehensive Health Care System for the Poor," *Brookings Review*, vol. 7 (Summer 1989), pp. 13–20.

6. Ibid., pp. 13–20.

7. Association of Maternal and Child Health Programs, "Information on Public Health Prenatal Programs," Washington, August 1990, p. 1.

8. Bonnie Lefkowitz and Judy Rodgers, "Primary Care Service Delivery Programs—A Critical Element to Ensuring Access to Care," Department of Health and Human Services, Bureau of Health Care Delivery and Assistance, Rockville, Md., March 1990, p. 11.

9. National Association of Community Health Centers, *Community and Migrant Health Centers: Two Decades of Achievement* (Washington, 1987).

10. Congressional Research Service, "Appropriations for Selected Health Programs, FY 1980–FY 1990," 90-360 EPW (July 26, 1990), table 1, p. 3.

11. Lefkowitz and Rodgers, "Primary Care Service Delivery Programs," p. 11.

12. Congressional Research Service, *CRS Report for Congress: Appropriations for Selected Health Programs, FY 1980–FY 1990,* Report 90-360 EPW (Washington, 1990).

13. States are involved in planning and coordination through cooperative agreements with the BHCDA. Also, many state maternal and child health programs supplement community health center funding with grants for maternal, infant, and child care.

14. National Association of Community Health Centers, "Congressional Briefing on the National Health Service Corps," Washington, February 2, 1990.

15. U.S. General Accounting Office (GAO), *National Health Service Corps: Program Unable to Meet Need for Physicians in Underserved Areas,* GAO/HRD-90-128 (1990), p. 6.

16. On average, it takes a student seven years to complete medical school and residency training. Thus reductions in the NHSC budget that began in 1981 did not begin to have a significant effect on the numbers of physicians available for placement until many years later. Ibid., table 1, p. 5.

17. Despite state subsidies of more than $2.5 billion for medical education during the 1987–88 school year, only an extremely small percentage of these funds were tied to some service obligation. Committee on Energy and Commerce, *Report on National Health Service Corps Revitalization Amendments of 1990,* to accompany H.R. 4487, Report 101-642 (GPO, July 1990), p. 17.

18. National Association of Community Health Centers, "Congressional Briefing."

19. Again, though not directly responsible for the administration of the program, states are involved through primary care cooperative agreements with the BHCDA.

20. This section draws heavily from *Federal Programs Affecting Children and Their Families, 1990,* Committee Print, House Select Committee on Children, Youth, and Families, 101 Cong. 2 sess. (GPO, 1990), pp. 203–04.

21. *Budget of the United States, Fiscal Year 1992,* pt. 4, p. 631.

22. The WIC target population includes low-income and nutritionally at risk pregnant women, postpartum women (up to six months after delivery if not breastfeeding), breastfeeding women (up to twelve months after delivery), infants up to 1 year old, and children up to 5 years old.

23. Mathematica Policy Research, Inc., *The Savings in Medicaid Costs for Newborns and Their Mothers from Prenatal Participation in the WIC Program* (U.S. Department of Agriculture, October 1990), vol. 1, p. 12.

24. Ibid.

25. Conversation with Stefan Harvey, Center on Budget and Policy Priorities, September 18, 1990.

26. Alan Guttmacher Institute, *Blessed Events and the Bottom Line: Financing Maternity Care in the United States* (New York, 1987), p. 36.

27. Bureau of Health Care Delivery and Assistance, "The Bureau's Unique Role," Health Resources and Services Administration, Washington, December 1988, p. 16.

28. Roger A. Reynolds, "Improving Access to Health Care among the Poor—The Neighborhood Health Center Experience," *Milbank Memorial Fund Quarterly: Health and Society*, no. 54 (Winter 1976), pp. 47–82; and G. Sparer and L. M. Okada, "Chronic Conditions and Physician Use Patterns in Ten Urban Poverty Areas," *Medical Care*, vol. 12 (July 1974), pp. 549–60.

29. National Commission to Prevent Infant Mortality, *One-Stop Shopping: The Road to Healthy Mothers and Children* (Washington, 1991).

30. Lefkowitz and Rodgers, "Primary Care Service Delivery Programs," p. 16.

31. In a comprehensive review of outreach programs for prenatal care, not limited to those in federally funded projects, the Institute of Medicine concluded that the effects of these efforts are mixed. In particular, it noted that many outreach efforts are undertaken without first making certain that the basic maternity care system is accessible and responsive to the patient's needs. Institute of Medicine, *Prenatal Care*, pp. 10–13.

32. Vince Hutchins and Charlotte Walch, "Meeting Minority Health Needs through Special MCH Projects," *Public Health Reports*, vol. 104 (November–December 1989), pp. 621–25. In another program funded by the Bureau of Maternal and Child Health, in Hood, Oregon, the El Nino Sano Project strives to bring unserved children of Mexican migrant farm workers into contact with well-child and other preventive health services, largely by using Spanish-speaking health educators. Hutchins and Walch, "Meeting Minority Needs through Special MCH Projects," pp. 621–25. Several C/MHCs in Pennsylvania which sponsor lay home visiting programs have reported that the rates of prenatal visit compliance, the return rate for postpartum care, returns for routine pediatric care, attendance at prenatal and parenting classes, compliance with family planning appointments, and WIC registration all improved. Natalie Lefkovich and David Webb, *Lay Home Visiting: An Integrated Approach to Prenatal and Postpartum Care—The Final Report and Evaluation* (Health Federation of Philadelphia, 1991).

33. Lefkowitz and Rodgers, "Primary Care Service Delivery Programs," p. 17.

34. Louise M. Okada and Thomas T. H. Wan, "Impact of Community Health Centers and Medicaid on the Use of Health Services," *Public Health Reports*, vol. 95 (November–December 1980), pp. 520–35.

35. Bureau of Health Care Delivery and Assistance, "The Bureau's Unique Role," p. 21.

36. Mark Schlesinger and Karl Kronebusch, "The Failure of Prenatal Care Policy for the Poor," *Health Affairs*, vol. 9 (Winter 1990), pp. 91–111.

37. Fred Goldman and Michael Grossman, "The Impact of Public Health Policy: The Care of Community Health Centers," Working Paper 1020 (New York: National Bureau of Economic Research, November 1982).

38. Leon Gordis, "Effectiveness of Comprehensive Care Programs in Preventing Rheumatic Fever," *New England Journal of Medicine*, vol. 290 (August 16, 1973), pp. 330–36.

CHAPTER SEVEN

1. It should be noted that counties and cities provide significant funding in some states.

2. *Budget of the United States Government, Fiscal Year 1992*, pt. 1, p. 2.

APPENDIX A

1. Congressional Research Service (CRS), *Medicaid Source Book: Background Data and Analysis*, Committee Print, prepared for the Subcommittee on Health and Environment of the House Committee on Energy and Commerce, 100 Cong. 2 sess. (November 1988), p. 5.

2. Ibid., p. 280.

3. Paul E. Peterson and Mark C. Rom, *Welfare Magnets* (Brookings, 1990), table 1-1, p. 8.

4. National Governors' Association, *Affording Access to Quality Care* (Washington, July 1986).

5. CRS, *Medicaid Source Book*, p. 207.

6. Ibid., p. 207.

7. Ibid., p. 208.

8. National Governors' Association, "State Coverage of Pregnant Women and Children, July 1990," Washington.

9. CRS, *Medicaid Source Book*, p. 208.

10. Ibid., p. 208.

11. Ibid., p. 208.

APPENDIX B

1. This appendix, including the tables, is drawn from the National Governors' Association, "State Coverage of Pregnant Women and Children, January 1991," Washington.

Panel Participants at the Brookings Conference

with their affiliations at the time of the conference

LAWTON CHILES, Chairman of the National Commission to Prevent Infant Mortality; former Senator from Florida

WARREN I. CIKINS, Senior staff member, Center for Public Policy Education, Brookings Institution

M. JOYCELYN ELDERS, Director, Arkansas Department of Health

WILLIS D. GOLDBECK, President, Washington Business Group on Health

ROBERT GREENSTEIN, Director, Center on Budget and Policy Priorities

EDMUND F. HAISLMAIER, Health care policy analyst, Heritage Foundation

IAN HILL, Senior policy analyst, National Governors' Association's Center for Policy Research

LAWRENCE S. LEWIN, President, Lewin/ICF, Inc.

DEBORAH LEWIS-IDEMA, Independent consultant

JAMES O. MASON, Assistant Secretary for Health, Public Health Service, U.S. Department of Health and Human Services

WILLIAM A. NISKANEN, Chairman, Cato Institute

JANET D. PERLOFF, Associate professor of health policy and health services research, College of Medicine, University of Illinois at Chicago

ALICE M. RIVLIN, Senior fellow, Economic Studies program, Brookings Institution

AARON SHIRLEY, Project director, Jackson-Hinds Comprehensive Health Center

REED TUCKSON, Commissioner of Public Health, District of Columbia Government

JOSHUA M. WIENER, Senior fellow, Economic Studies program, Brookings Institution

GAIL R. WILENSKY, Vice-president, Division of Health Affairs, and director, Center for Health Affairs, Project HOPE

Other Conference Participants

with their affiliations at the time of the conference

Rhoda Abrams
*U.S. Department of Health and
Human Services*

Loretta Alexander
*Arkansas Department of Human
Services*

John W. Alquest
*Kansas Department of Social and
Rehabilitative Services*

Dottie Andrews
Parent Care, Inc.

Dennis Andrulis
*National Association of Public
Hospitals*

Ross Anthony
*U.S. Department of Health and
Human Services*

Katherine L. Armstrong
*U.S. Department of Health and
Human Services*

Carolyn H. Asbury
Robert Wood Johnson Foundation

Cheryl F. Austein
*U.S. Department of Health and
Human Services*

David A. Austin
*Department of Medical Assistance
Services, Virginia*

Gordon B. Avery
*Children's Hospital National Medical
Center*

Donna Mahaffey Barber
*Florida Department of Health and
Rehabilitative Services*

Lawrence Bartlett
Health Systems Research, Inc.

Winston Barton
*Kansas Department of Social and
Rehabilitative Services*

Terry W. Beck
Mississippi State Department of Health

Donna C. Becker
*Department of Health and Mental
Hygiene, Maryland*

Ev Beguin, Jr.
National Perinatal Association

David D. Bellis
U.S. General Accounting Office

Mimi Bernardin
Office of Senator Bill Bradley

Susan Biggs
*Organization for Obstetric,
Gynecologic, and Neonatal Nurses*

Rachel Block
New York State Assembly

Karen Bodenhorn
Capitol Associates, Inc.

Ross Bonner
*National Association of Community
Health Centers*

John J. Botti
Pennsylvania Perinatal Association

Frank W. Bowen
Pennsylvania Hospital

Mary C. Brecht
U.S. General Accounting Office

Paul Brenner
Children's Hospice International

Linda Bresolin
American Medical Association

Seiko Brodbeck
American Public Health Association

Sarah Brown
Institute of Medicine

Gretchen A. Brown
U.S. Department of Health and Human Services

Carola Bruflat
National Perinatal Association

Kathy J. Bryant
American College of Obstetricians and Gynecologists

Robert F. Byrnes
Tokos Medical Corporation

Susan M. Campell
American Academy of Pediatrics

Patricia A. Caplan
U.S. Department of Health and Human Services

J. Chris Carey
Department of Obstetrics and Gynecology, University of Oklahoma

Ronald H. Carlson
U.S. Department of Health and Human Services

Mary Ann Carlson
Montana Perinatal Association

Judy Castleman
Virginia Perinatal Association

Cathy Certner
Washington Business Group on Health

Debbie Chang
Office of Senator Donald Riegle

Janet Chapin
American College of Obstetricians and Gynecologists

Mary Ann Chestnut
Family Help, Inc.

Joseph A. Cislowski
National Commission on Children

Lori Cooper
Healthy Mothers, Healthy Babies

Tamara Copeland
Southern Regional Project on Infant Mortality

Carole L. Corbitt
American Academy of Pediatrics

Caroline Costle
Office of Congressman Robert Wise

Warren M. Crosby
Department of Obstetrics and Gynecology, University of Oklahoma

Marietta Cross
Montana Perinatal Association

Joni Cunningham
U.S. Department of Health and Human Services

Elizabeth Cusick
U.S. Department of Health and Human Services

Ezra Davidson, Jr.
Charles R. Drew University of Science and Medicine

Christopher Degraw
Office of Senator Tom Harkin

Sandra Donze
March of Dimes, Greater Baltimore

Sally Faith Dorfman
Commissioner of Health, Orange County, New York

Lorraine Driscoll
Citizen Action

Sara Ducey
Society for Nutrition Education

Michael Duffy
*U.S. Department of Health and
Human Services*

Nicholas Eberstadt
American Enterprise Institute

Jeannie Engel
Senate Special Committee on Aging

Scott Epstein
Blue Cross/Blue Shield Association

Alan Fairbank
Congressional Budget Office

Karen S. Fennell
American College of Nurse-Midwives

Amy Fine
*Center on Budget and Policy
Priorities*

Gerard J. Foye, Jr.
Connecticut Perinatal Association

Harriette B. Fox
Fox Health Policy Consultants

Julia Lopez Fueyo
Florida Perinatal Association

Anne K. Gauthier
Alpha Center

Mary Beth Gehl
Pennsylvania Perinatal Association

Richard C. Gilbert
American Public Health Association

Sue Ginsburg
Continental Health Care Association

Susan Givens
North Carolina Perinatal Association

J. William Godsby
U.S. General Accounting Office

Rachel Gold
Alan Guttmacher Institute

John J. Graham
*American College of Obstetricians
and Gynecologists*

Maureen Greer
*Institute for the Study of
Developmental Disabilities*

Janis Guerney
*U.S. Bipartisan Commission on
Comprehensive Health Care*

David M. Gute
Tufts University

Barbara Harness
American Hospital Association

Anne Harrison-Clark
March of Dimes

Marie L. Hart
Texas Perinatal Association

John V. Hartline
National Perinatal Association

Birt Harvey
American Academy of Pediatrics

Stephen Harvey
Center on Budget and Policy Priorities

Herman A. Hein
University of Iowa

Catherine A. Hess
*Association of Maternal and Child
Health Programs*

Robert R. Hillis
Oklahoma Perinatal Association

Elizabeth Hintz
National Association of Public Hospitals

William Mc. Hiscock
*U.S. Department of Health and
Human Services*

John Holahan
Urban Institute

William H. Hollinshead
Rhode Island Department of Health

Vince Hutchins
U.S. Department of Health and Human Services

Cassandra Joubert Jackson
Oklahoma Community Service Council

Timothy R. B. Johnson
American Association for Maternal and Neonatal Health

Larry O. Jones
National Perinatal Association

Joel Kallich
U.S. Department of Health and Human Services

Donald L. Kelley
Texas Department of Human Services

John J. Kelly
Pennsylvania Perinatal Association

Asta Kenney
Alan Guttmacher Institute

Woodie Kessel
U.S. Department of Health and Human Services

Janet L. Kline
Library of Congress

Marvin O. Kolb
American Academy of Pediatrics

Jane Koppelman
National Health Policy Forum

Ann M. Koontz
U.S. Department of Health and Human Services

Marian Lake
National Perinatal Association

Barbara Langer
Senate Committee on Finance

Jennifer Layman-Heitman
Food Research and Action Center

Barbara Lederer
Connecticut Department of Income Maintenance

Bonnie Lefkowitz
U.S. Department of Health and Human Services

Martha Lewis
Partners of the Americas

Joy M. Lewis
Virginia Perinatal Association

Susan Lieberman
Philadelphia Department of Public Health

Susan A. Lightfoot
American College of Obstetricians and Gynecologists

Joseph Liu
Children's Defense Fund

Carla Lunetta
American Nurses Association

Marty McGeein
National Council of Community Hospitals

Peggy McManus
McManus Health Policy, Inc.

Carol K. Mahan
National Perinatal Association

Barbara D. Matula
North Carolina Division of Medical Assistance

Adrienne Kirby McDonnell
Pennsylvania Perinatal Association

Kathy E. Means
Office of Senator David Durenberger

Calvin Michaels
Burlington Industries, Inc.

C. Arden Miller
University of North Carolina

Michael L. Millman
Institute of Medicine, National
Academy of Sciences

Kathryn Moore
American College of Obstetricians
and Gynecologists

Lyn Mortimer
Carnegie Corporation of New York

Paul Newacheck
University of California at San
Francisco

Herbert W. Nickens
Association of American Colleges

Alice Novitsky
March of Dimes

Elizabeth J. Noyes
American Academy of Pediatrics

Ann O'Sullivan
University of Pennsylvania

Paul Offner
Ohio Department of Health and
Human Services

Peter Paulsen
Southern Regional Project on Infant
Mortality

Mary Ella Payne
Office of Senator John D. Rockefeller

Warren H. Pearse
American College of Obstetricians
and Gynecologists

Susie F. Peden
South Carolina Perinatal Association

Miriam E. Phields
U.S. Conference of Mayors

Mary Plaska
National Association of Community
Health Centers

Donald Poppke
U.S. Department of Health and
Human Services

Renee Rappanart
Office of Senator Richard Bryan

Nancy Rawding
National Association of County
Health Officials

Gary B. Redding
Georgia Department of Medical
Assistance

Irwin Redlener
New York Hospital–Cornell Medical
Center

James R. Ricciuti
Senate Committee on Finance

Julius B. Richmond
Harvard University

Robert C. Rinaldi
American Medical Association

Jack Rodgers
Congressional Budget Office

Martha Romans
American Hospital Association

Harriet Rose
Perinatal Council of Northeastern
California

Julie Rovner
Congressional Quarterly

Lesley M. Russell
House Energy and Commerce
Committee

Jeff Sanders
Senate Budget Committee

Emily Santer
U.S. Department of Health and
Human Services

Mona Sarfaty
Senate Labor and Human Resources
Committee

Donald Schiff
American Academy of Pediatrics

Andy Schneider
House Subcommittee on Health and Environment

Lisbeth B. Schorr
Harvard University

Rachel Schwartz
National Perinatal Information Center

Mary A. Scoblic
Michigan Department of Public Health

Linda Sizelove
U.S. Department of Health and Human Services

Sheila M. Smythe
U.S. General Accounting Office

Elliot Sogol
Glaxo, Inc.

Michelle Solloway
Intergovernmental Health Policy Project

Judy G. Sommers
University of South Florida

Sheila Smolens Sorkin
Pennsylvania Perinatal Association

Carol M. Statuto
House Select Committee on Children, Youth, and Families

Deborah Steelman
Epstein, Becker and Green

Sharon Stout
Economic Policy Institute

James E. Strain
American Academy of Pediatrics

Laura Summer
Center on Budget and Policy Priorities

Eleanor S. Szanton
National Center for Clinical Infant Programs

James R. Tallon, Jr.
New York State Assembly

Patricia Tompkins
Commission on Public Health

Sidney Trieger
U.S. Department of Health and Human Services

Donna Vivio
National Perinatal Association

Anne Weiss
Senate Finance Committee

Kenneth R. Weiss
New York Times Regional Newspapers

Aileen Whitfill
Children's Defense Fund

Peters D. Willson
National Association of Children's Hospitals and Related Institutions

Margaret S. Wilson
Eastern Connecticut State University

Shelley D. Yanoff
Philadelphia Citizens for Children and Youth

Azzie Yound
Kansas Department of Health and Environment

Phyllis M. Zucker
U.S. Department of Health and Human Services

Kathryn Zuckerman
U.S. Department of Health and Human Services